Do Your Own
BOOKKEEPING

Do Your Own BOOKKEEPING

MAX PULLEN

KOGAN
PAGE

First published in Great Britain in 1988 by
Kogan Page Ltd, 120 Pentonville Road, London N1 9JN

Reprinted with revisions 1994, 1995

British Library Cataloguing in Publication Data
Pullen, Max
   Do your own bookkeeping.
   1. Great Britain. Small firms. Book-
   keeping – Manuals
   I. Title
   657'.2
ISBN 1-85091-711-6
ISBN 1-85091-710-8 Pbk

Printed and bound in Great Britain by
Biddles Ltd, Guildford and King's Lynn

Contents

Introduction

Although a successful business may be founded on acumen – the perception of an opportunity and the exploiting of it – to grow and prosper it needs sound financial planning and control.

Many a bright idea develops into a successful business. Regrettably, many more fail to mature. Often the basic idea is uncommercial or is pursued without adequate financial backing.

It may take even a year or two to recognise that running a business involves the combination of several skills – not just the application of one particular skill. Marketing, selling, product design and development, production and financial planning are all equally involved.

Too frequently a business becomes caught up in problems which could have been avoided by initial training. Then no time can be found to get away, even for a day or two, to learn the skills which have not been mastered.

Perhaps one of the most neglected skills is bookkeeping, that seemingly unglamorous occupation which is thought to be all very well for people who like that sort of thing, but not for practical people. Some feel, misguidedly, that the bank balance is the indicator of profit.

It is to dispel that fallacy that this book has been written. Bookkeeping is interesting when one gets to know it. The accounts provide the business with its navigation chart. It is as essential for a business to plan and plot its course as it is for a ship or an aeroplane. Business plans are not star-gazing, they are forethought without which too many businesses fail, big and small.

Yet it is only a matter of clear thinking and it is hoped that the following pages will at least demonstrate the fact.

The systems and procedures which are explained aim to introduce bookkeeping in a practical way to those with little prior knowledge. But they are then developed for the preparation of final accounts for submission to an accountant for audit.

Although sole traders are not legally obliged to prepare accounts, they are strongly advised to do so in order to make certain they have a correct view of the state of their affairs and to ensure that their tax assessment is not excessive. Limited companies, on the other hand, have a legal obligation to present their shareholders with accounts which have been audited by an accountant with recognised qualifications and to file their accounts with the Registrar of Companies.

In either case the keeping of records and books of account as described in the following pages will not only provide the business with up-to-date management information but also enable the accountant speedily to prepare official accounts giving independent confirmation of the state of the business.

The Inspector of Taxes will require such accounts either in the form of a Statement of Income and Expenditure or of a Profit and Loss Account upon which to base his assessment of liability to tax. Taxation is a specialist area beyond the scope of day-to-day bookkeeping and financial control. Businesses are assessed to tax according to rules laid down by the Income and Corporation Taxes Act 1970 and subsequent annual Finance Acts. Since the rules are liable to legislative changes, taxation is a matter on which the accountant's advice must be sought.

Suffice to say at this stage that sole traders and partners pay income tax on the profits of their business but individuals are able to claim deduction of personal allowances to which they are entitled. They do not pay tax on money which they draw from the business because these amounts are, in fact, payments to them of part of the profit on which their tax liability will be assessed.

Limited companies pay Corporation Tax on their profits. A limited company, however, is regarded at law as a separate entity – like another person – and it can pay salaries to its directors and must deduct income tax under PAYE rules as with all employee remuneration. Such salaries are deductible when arriving at the profit on which the company pays Corporation Tax.

The profits of the company, in effect, belong to the shareholders who vote at an Annual General Meeting on the distribution of that profit as a dividend from which income tax will be deemed to have been deducted by the company.

At some stage consideration should be given to computerisation of accounts, but such a step should not be taken until there is a sound understanding of accounting principles. Computers and even good software packages, of which there are very many available, must be used with understanding if erroneous or misleading data are to be avoided. Their introduction should be assessed with the co-operation and guidance of the accountant. Computerised accounts have not been dealt with in these pages which concentrate on providing a basic understanding of bookkeeping and accountancy.

Chapter 1
Basic Bookkeeping

The purpose

1. To show the state of affairs of the business and whether it is profitable or not.
2. To provide, regularly, simple statistics as an instant guide to the business performance.
3. To provide a record of past activities and a basis for planning the future.
4. To avoid the overpayment of tax.

The treatment in the books of some items, such as loans, hire-purchase agreements and leases, can be complicated and need professional assistance, but the following notes and illustrations should lead to an understanding of the general principles of bookkeeping and financial control.

Buying and selling

BUYING   Goods for resale
Materials for production of goods
Services such as power, telephone, etc
People's time – wages

SELLING   Goods bought for resale
Goods produced
Time – providing service to customers

Bookkeeping is about recording the movement of money caused by buying and selling.

Two books are needed:

1. Cash Book in which to record receipts and payments made in cash.
2. Bank Book in which to record deposits and withdrawals from the bank account.

Cash is both cash and cheques. There will be a cash-box or a till and a bank account.

The cash and bank books are the heart of bookkeeping. As the business develops other books or records will be useful. If you are making sales or purchases on credit terms you will need two more books:

Sales Book
Purchases Book

For a complete accounting system you will need to keep records of:

Wages – if you employ people
Stocks – of raw materials and goods for sale
Fixed assets – purchases and disposals
Value added tax – if you are VAT registered

There are several proprietary manual systems of bookkeeping obtainable from stationers' shops. Mostly, however, they are appropriate only to businesses with daily cash takings and payments and few dealings in cheques. Because they are based upon a page for each week it is cumbersome to monitor or to analyse monthly income and expenditures and most difficult to agree or reconcile the system with the bank statement.

There is not usually any clear or simple way of recording sales and purchases on credit so that it can be very time-consuming to prepare statements showing trading results, the state of affairs of the business or financial accounts.

Analysis books, such as 'Guildhall' or 'Cathedral' are obtainable from most stationers. They are published in a wide range of rulings with up to 26 cash columns. One can choose books for use as cash books, purchase books, sales books, etc each with the number of columns required by the particular business. These columns can be used to analyse income and expenditure as is most appropriate to the needs of the business.

The suggestions which follow are based upon the use of such analysis books.

The cash books
Cash and bank transactions can be recorded in one book and many accountants do this. It involves using a book with two adjacent columns headed 'Cash' and 'Bank', ie:

RECEIPTS				·	PAYMENTS			
Date	Received from	Amount		Date	Paid to	Amount		
		Cash	Bank			Cash	Bank	

Each time cash is paid into the bank the amount has to be written on the receipts side in the bank column and on the payments side in the Cash column to record the movement of cash. Similarly, two entries must be made when cash is drawn from the bank. This method can lead to confusion. It can, perhaps, be better understood if two books are used – a cash book and a bank book and the bookkeeping is made to mirror what happens in practice. When money passes from the cash box to the bank (or vice versa) it is recorded in the Cash Book as a payment (money going out) and in the bank book as a receipt (money going in). The cash book is a record of all that happens in the cash box and the Bank Book is a record of all that happens in the account at the bank.

This method has two other advantages:

1. It makes checking of the bank statement simpler.
2. It assists the accountant, when preparing accounts, to verify receipts and payments by cash or cheque. (It saves his time and may well reduce his fee.)

If the amount of VAT is not shown separately on your bills for purchases or sales it must be calculated.

Example:

If VAT rate is 17.5 per cent, your payment or receipt equals 117.5 per cent of the price excluding VAT. Thus VAT = 17.5/117.5ths of the amount paid or received.

Retailers can adopt a special scheme by which they can avoid this necessity. Details can be obtained from the VAT office.

13

Trace the functions of buying and selling and the recording that is required

BUYING. Goods may be bought for cash or on credit.

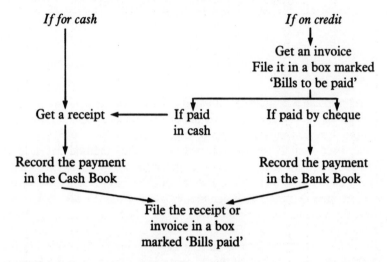

Note: Invoices in the box 'Bills to be paid' represent money owed by the business.

SELLING. Goods may be sold for cash or on credit.

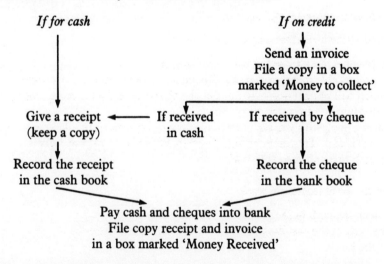

Note: Copy invoices in the box 'Money to collect' represent money owed to the business.

Cash Book

RECEIPTS							PAYMENTS						
Date		Received from	Total Rec'd	VAT %	VAT	Net	Date		Paid to	Total paid	VAT %	VAT	Net

Handling cash and the Cash Book

Record all cash received and all cash spent.

If possible use a till fitted with a till roll; *or*
use a lockable metal cash box and keep in it a hard-backed book (one which will not get dog-eared or fall apart) and record all receipts into and payments from the box; *and*
carry a book with you for use when receiving or paying cash while out at work each day – deduct total payments from receipts, pay balance to cash box and record in book.

Each day or at least each week:

Check the cash in the till agrees with the till roll;
the cash in the cash box agrees with the balance in the book
in the box.

Empty the till and the cash box and pay the cash into the bank.
The takings (less spending) shown on the till roll and in the cash box

book will be seen – to the penny – in your paying-in book and on your bank statement – indisputable evidence of the accuracy of your books.

It is usually advisable to keep a float in the cash box or the till to meet inevitable needs. So, before balancing the Cash Book or till and paying cash into the bank, keep back a certain sum and record it on the till roll or in the Cash Book on the payments side as 'Balance carried forward'. Record this balance on the new till roll or the receipts side of the new page of the Cash Book as 'Balance brought forward'.

Keep receipts for all payments whenever you can and copies of receipts given to customers. File them in boxes marked 'Bills paid' and 'Money received'. Staple each week together so that they can be checked easily with your books.

If you are usually paid by cheque and only occasionally receive cash you pay any cash received into the bank using a separate paying-in slip so that it can be identified on your bank statement. You must record on the paying-in slip who it was from. Your cash box will then be used only for small purchases and incidental expenses. So keep it on an imprest system, that is:

Draw from bank an appropriate float – say £50 – and put that cash in the box.

Record all expenses in the Cash Book.

At the end of the week – total the expenses and draw that sum from the bank to reimburse box.

The box will now contain £50 again.

Note: At any time the total of expenses plus the cash in the box must equal £50.

Writing up the Cash Book

Enter receipts on the left and payments on the right-hand side of the book kept in the cash box and each day, or at least each week, add up the total receipts and payments and strike a balance which is paid into the bank and, of course, entered as a receipt in the bank book. Because this entry involves both receipts and payments it will need special treatment in the Bank Book. The payment into the bank will be shown as a receipt in the Bank Book and analysed to 'Cash Sales' but the amount of sales will obviously be understated by the amount of the expenditure which has been deducted. To correct this, write in the Bank Book what is called a 'Contra entry' – put the total amount of expenses in the 'Cash Sales' column which will bring the sales to the right amount and put the expenses into the appropriate column on the payment side. Alternatively, the correction can be made by using the Journal (see Journal – page 54 and illustrations pages 15 (Cash Book) and 56 (Journal).

Handling the bank

Enter receipts on the left-hand side and payments on the right.

Amounts paid in

From each paying-in book counterfoil enter the date and the amount paid in into the Total Received column. Enter in the next column any discount allowed and into the Total column the sum of the amount received plus the discount.

If the money has been received from a credit customer, copy the total into the column headed CR Sales. (CR = Credit.) This is the amount which must be written against the invoice in the Sales Book and the two amounts must agree if the invoice has been paid in full.

If the money has been received from cash sales, ie when paying in money collected from the till or cash box, enter, from the cash book, the amount of VAT into the VAT column and net amount (TOTAL minus VAT) into the Cash Sales column.

If the money has come from some other source – say a grant or a rebate – copy the total into one of the spare columns and give that column an appropriate heading. Remember to separate any VAT if it applies.

Amounts withdrawn

From each cheque book counterfoil enter each cheque date, cheque number and the amount into the Total Paid column. Enter in the next column any discount allowed and into the Total column the sum of the cheque amount plus the discount.

If money has been paid for a credit purchase, copy the Total into the column headed CR Purch. This is the amount which must be written against the invoice in the Purchases Book and the two amounts must agree if the invoice has been paid in full.

If the cheque is for the payment of wages or salaries, PAYE or the quarterly payment of VAT to HM Customs, copy the total into the appropriate column.

If the cheque is for purchases not made on credit, enter the VAT involved in the VAT column and the net amount (total minus VAT) in a column above which you can write an appropriate heading according to the nature of the expense.

By keeping a running total of receipts and payments you can calculate your bank balance every day. Remember to allow for Standing Orders and Direct Debits.

Every month. When you have entered standing orders from the bank statement, add up all columns on each page and see that they cross-cast.

Bank Book

Left-hand side

RECEIPTS

Date	Received from	Total Rec'd	Disc Allowed	Total	CR sales	Cash Sales							VAT %	VAT

Right-hand side

PAYMENTS

Date	Chq No	Paid to	Total Paid	Disc Rec'd	Total	CR Purch	Wages	Salaries	PAYE	HM Customs			Fixed Assets	Draw'gs	Sundry	VAT %	VAT

You then know your total receipts and payments for the month and you have an analysis of them. Calculate the balance at the bank, being the difference between receipts plus opening balance (or minus opening overdraft) and payments.

Bank reconciliation

The bank statement shows only the deposits and cheques which have been cleared through the bank by the date on which the statement was issued. The bank statement will also record standing orders and direct debits which you have authorised the bank to execute but will not have written in your Bank Book. Finally, the bank statement records bank charges levied by the bank.

To explain the difference between the bank balance and the statement and that in the Bank Book, each entry on the statement must be checked off against the Bank Book. This will prove the accuracy of both documents as well as identify the differences.

The entries on the bank statement for bank charges, standing orders and direct debits must be copied into the Bank Book and the new Bank Book balance reconciled with the statement.

	£
Balance per bank statement	
Add: deposits in bank book but not on statement	
	————
Deduct: cheques in bank book but not on statement	
	————
Balance per bank book	£
	════

Credit purchases

When you receive credit from a supplier, instead of requiring you to pay on delivery, he will send you an *invoice*, quoting the terms of payment. Make sure that the invoice is correctly priced and that you have received the goods or services and are satisfied with them. If not, dispute it.

File the invoice – a purchase invoice – in a box marked 'Bills to be paid'.

On the due date for payment the invoice may be paid in cash or by cheque. (Always try to pay in time to benefit from any discount allowed for prompt payment.)

Write on the invoice the date and method of payment (cash or cheque), the cheque number and the amount and write 'Paid' on the invoice. Note also any discount taken.

If *paid in cash* from the cash box, write the payment in the cash book.

If *paid by cheque*, remember to fill in the counterfoil stating to whom the cheque was made out, the amount of the cheque and also the amount of discount so that the two amounts add up to the total of the invoice.

If *only part of the invoice has been paid* (ie, an instalment of rates) file the invoice back into the box 'Bills to be paid' so that it reminds you that further payments will have to be made.

If *the invoice has been completely paid* file it in a box marked 'Bills paid'.

Note: Some invoices (perhaps rates and rent) will be paid by standing order or by direct debit to which you have consented. This is money going out of your account for which you will not have written a cheque and you will have to pick these up when you get your bank statement.

Use of credit cards

When you use your credit cards (Visa, Access etc) to make purchases you are making purchases on credit. Treat the credit card slip, of which you are given a copy, just like a supplier's purchase invoice. File it in the 'Bills to be paid' box. When you receive the bill from the credit card company, extract the relevant slips from your box, check them against the bill, staple them to it and refile it in the 'Bills to be paid' box. When you make the payment, write 'Paid' on the bill and take all the other actions described above just as you would do with any supplier's invoice.

Suppliers' statements

Some suppliers will send you each month a statement of your account on which they will list all the invoices which they say you have not paid.

Treat these like your credit card bills, that is extract from your 'Bills to be paid' box all the invoices shown on the statement and check both that the statement is correct and that you have not paid the invoices. If you have paid some, alter the statement and write the date paid against such invoices. The others you can staple to the amended statement and refile in the 'Bills to be paid' file. You then treat it like any other invoice

21

INVOICE

A & B TRADERS
14 South Street, Newcastle Upon Tyne NE3 1BT

VAT Reg. No. 111 2222 33   Date:

Customer:

Description	Quantity	Price		£	
				VAT	
				Total £	

Terms of payment: Net 30 days from date of Invoice.
Interest at 2% per month will be charged
on overdue accounts.

and go through the procedure described above when the time comes when you want to make a payment.

An important factor in running any business is knowing how much the business owes to its suppliers for goods and services purchased on credit and also how much credit customers owe to the business.

Being allowed credit by suppliers is equivalent to borrowing money free of interest and is a privilege which must not be abused. By the same token, allowing credit to customers is equivalent to lending them money free of interest and there is obviously a limit to the credit that can be allowed.

To establish how much the business owes or is owed involves adding up all the invoices in the 'Bills to be paid' box and the 'Money to collect' box, and deducting the smaller from the larger sum. In the process the invoices will probably have to be listed and when there are perhaps 20 or more invoices this can be tiresome and time-consuming. At this stage it is worthwhile to start using a Purchases Book and a Sales Book to record the invoices and mark them off as they are paid. The unpaid ones then show up clearly.

If the sales of the business require registration for VAT (the annual threshold is announced in the Budget), the Purchases Book and Sales Book become essential in order to establish easily how much VAT has been paid on purchases and is recoverable from HM Customs and Excise and how much VAT has been charged to customers on sales invoices which is the amount owed to HM Customs and Excise.

These books have other advantages within the bookkeeping system when it comes to writing up accounts to show whether the business is profitable. At this stage it is necessary to know the cost of all purchases and the value of all sales, whether paid for or not. Instead of having to add up all the 'Bills paid' and 'Bills to pay' the Purchases Book can more easily provide this data if it is ruled off at the end of each month and the monthly totals added up. Similarly, the Sales Book, ruled off and added up each month, can easily provide the monthly total value of sales invoices.

Credit sales

Before you agree to allow credit make sure that your customer is reliable. When sales are made on credit, instead of paying at the time of delivery or at the completion of a job, an *invoice* or a bill must be written out and sent to the customer as soon as possible.

Do not delay sending the invoice – the sooner it is sent the sooner it may be paid.

A sales invoice can be written on a form specially printed for you, which creates a good businesslike impression, but can be written on a page of a duplicate book obtainable from any stationers. But the following conditions must apply to every invoice.

It must be pre-numbered – each invoice or page of the duplicate book must be numbered by the printer so that each invoice is accounted for and there are no gaps in the sequence of numbers. If one is spoilt, do not destroy it, write 'cancelled' across it and keep it to prove that it has not been lost or omitted from your books.

It must be in duplicate so that you have a copy from which your books can be checked and particularly so that you know how much money to collect and can make sure you get paid.

The original of the invoice is sent to the customer. The copy is to be filed in a box marked 'Money to collect'.

The invoice should have the Terms of Payment written on it so that the customer knows when payment is due, ie,

payment in 30 days from date of invoice; or
end of month following month of invoice; or
2½ per cent discount allowed for payment in 7 days; or
whatever terms you wish to apply

Chase debts; have a programme for debt collection and stick to it rigidly. By way of example:

If payment is   7 days overdue – send a written but polite reminder;
      30 days overdue – write a letter threatening legal action if not paid;
      50 days overdue – write a warning that legal action will be taken if not paid in seven days;
      57 days overdue – refer the account to your solicitor for collection.

STOP TRADING WITH CUSTOMERS WHO DO NOT PAY ON TIME OR REGULARLY.

If your customer is reliable but has cash-flow problems which he cannot avoid, agree special terms with him which will suit both parties and, if necesary, increase your price to allow for longer credit. After all, it is your money invested in him.

When the money is received
1. Write 'Paid' on your copy of the invoice with the date and whether paid in cash or by cheque.

2. If cash is received either put it in cash box and enter it in the cash book or pay the cash into the bank and keep the paying-in book counterfoil.
3. If a cheque is received, pay it into the bank and keep the paying-in counterfoil. *Remember* to write on the counterfoil who the money has been received from and the amount, together with any discount allowed so that the two accounts add up to the total of the invoice.
4. *Refile* your copy of the invoice in a box marked 'Money received'.
5. *Bank cheques daily* to ensure quick clearance and crediting to your account.

Purchases Book for credit purchases

Every purchase invoice in the 'Bills to pay', box must be written into the Purchase Book. Enter the date, supplier's name, the total of the invoice, the VAT and the net total excluding VAT.

The total (excluding VAT) should then be analysed to the appropriate column according to the nature of the expense involved, for example: raw materials, goods for resale, rent, rates, insurance, telephone. Select the headings against which you want to analyse expenses according to what is most appropriate to your business.

As each invoice is paid it is marked off in the columns – amount paid (including discount), date paid and method of payment (cash or cheque).

At the end of each month add up the columns to provide the total amount of credit purchases during the month and the analysis to types of expense. The analysis will help you to watch and control your costs.

Add up the total amount of invoices unpaid to obtain how much you owe and check that each unpaid invoice in the book is in fact in the 'Bills to be paid' box awaiting payment. Remember to check earlier months for invoices still unpaid and take care to avoid long standing debts which might give rise to disquiet among your suppliers.

Sales Book for credit sales

Every sales invoice in the 'Money to collect' box must be recorded in the Sales Book and they must all be entered in numerical order. If one is incorrectly written out, do not destroy it, but write 'cancelled' across it, file it and record it in the Sales Book as 'cancelled'. Enter the date and number of each invoice, the invoice total, the VAT and the net total excluding VAT.

The total (excluding VAT) can be analysed over the analysis columns appropriately headed according to sources of income. By this means

Purchases Book

PURCHASES																		
Date		Supplier	Inv Total	VAT	NET	Am't Paid	Date	Method										
		Totals																

Sales Book

		SALES																	
Date	Inv No	Customer	Inv Total	VAT	NET	Am't Paid	Date	Method											
		Totals																	

sales could be analysed between the various products sold or, if preferred, between various geographical regions or types of market outlet, such as wholesale or retail.

As payments are received from customers, mark off against each invoice the amount paid (including discount) date paid and method of payment (cash or cheque). At the end of each month add up the columns to provide the total amount of credit sales during the month and the analysis to products, regions or markets. The analysis will be a useful guide to checking your sales policy.

Add up the total amount of invoices unpaid to obtain how much your customers owe you and check that each unpaid invoice is in the 'Money to collect' box. Remember to check earlier months for unpaid invoices and set debt collection procedures in motion to chase slow payers.

Value added tax (VAT)

As soon as your sales in any quarter or in any year reach the prescribed amount you are, by law, obliged to register for VAT.

You must then add a charge for VAT on all your invoices to your customers and make a quarterly VAT return to HM Customs & Excise showing the total amount of your sales invoiced during the quarter and the amount of VAT charged on those invoices. You must enclose a cheque paying the VAT to HM Customs & Excise. The return also includes a statement of your total purchases during the quarter and the amount of VAT charged to you on those purchases. The amount of VAT you have been charged (INPUT VAT) can be deducted from the amount you have charged out to your customers (OUTPUT VAT) and you need to make out your cheque for the net amount only.

Sometimes, when you buy expensive machinery or equipment, or if you make export sales on which you do not have to charge VAT, HM Customs & Excise will have to pay you if your INPUT VAT exceeds your OUTPUT VAT.

Therefore; all your cash books and your bank book should have three cash columns on the receipts side and on the payments side. These columns will be used to show, in respect of all receipts and payments:

the total amount of each receipt or payment;
the amount of VAT included in the total; and
the amount excluding VAT

Each month, and each quarter, you will then be able to add up the columns to provide, quite simply, the figures needed for your VAT return.

Value added tax Summary

OUTPUT TAX	Month	Month	Month	TOTAL		
Sales						
					VAT RETURN	
Totals					Box	1

INPUT TAX	Month	Month	Month	TOTAL		
Purchases						
Cash						
Bank						
Totals					Box	5

	NET TAX	Payable or Receivable		Box	8

OUTPUT (before VAT)	Month	Month	Month	TOTAL		
Sales						
Totals					Box	9

INPUT (before VAT)	Month	Month	Month	TOTAL		
Purchases						
Cash						
Bank						
Totals					Box	10

29

HM Customs & Excise will visit you to check your invoices for sales and purchases to make sure that the correct VAT has been charged and the VAT rules obeyed and that your return is accurate. There are severe penalties for not obeying the rules and for making late returns, so keep your books in good order and your files of sales and purchase invoices or receipts.

Even if your sales are below the VAT limits you can register for VAT voluntarily. Sometimes it can be wise to do so when, for example, most of your customers and your suppliers are VAT registered. When you are registered your prices or charges will have to include VAT but, because you will be able to recover the VAT you have paid on your purchases, you may end up better off. Check out the situation and seek advice.

By completing the VAT summary each month it is possible to calculate how much is owed to HM Customs & Excise (total output tax minus total input tax).

Since this money does not belong to the business and will later have to be paid over, it can be put to one side in a deposit account so that:

1. Interest is being earned on someone else's money.
2. The money is available when the demand for tax payment is received.

Bookkeeping entries
When tax is paid, the cheque will naturally be entered in the Bank Book as are all other cheques and analysed to a column headed 'HM Customs & Excise'.

When input tax exceeds output tax and HM Customs & Excise make a repayment, their cheque will be banked and written into the Bank Book.

Personal ledgers for debtors and creditors

When several invoices are issued to a customer each month or received each month from a supplier it becomes difficult to be certain of the state of the account, ie, how much is outstanding. At this stage it is advisable to open a *Debtors Ledger* for customers' accounts and for suppliers a *Creditors Ledger*.

Each time a sales invoice is raised and written into the Sales Book it is also written into the Debtors Ledger in which each debtor (or customer) is allocated a separate page. Similarly, each time a cheque or cash is received from a debtor and written into the Bank Book, it is entered on the credit side of the debtor's account. A page or account need not be written up for every customer – perhaps only those with whom frequent business is done, but to make the ledger complete open a page for 'Sundries' to which is posted every invoice or cheque relating to customers not requiring a separate page.

It may well be that it becomes advisable to use a page or account for most customers and suppliers. At this stage the personal ledgers can take over from the Purchases Book and Sales Book as a means of establishing how much is owed to or by the business.

Clearly, a list of the balances on each of the accounts in the Debtors Ledger is a list of money owed to the business. The total of this list must be reconciled as follows:

List of debtors at the end of the previous month.
Add   Sales for the month as shown in the Sales Book.
Minus   Cash or cheques received from customers as shown in the Cash Book and Bank Book.
Equals Total of the list of debtors extracted from the ledger at the end of the month.

If there is a difference it means that an invoice or cheque has been omitted, overlooked or entered wrongly, and the error must be found and corrected. Differences can arise when discounts are involved and not properly recorded in the Cash or Bank Book.

A creditors ledger operates in the same way as a Debtors Ledger using purchase invoices and the Bank/Cash Book and a page for each supplier.

It is important to examine all the accounts in both ledgers each month and satisfy yourself that the balances are a true record of what is owed. Suppliers' accounts can be checked with statements received from them and any differences ironed out. If corrections have to be made they are made by using the Journal.

Also examine the balance on each account and determine which invoices are outstanding and for how long it has been so. If the payment terms are 'monthly' a firm reminder must be sent to all that are two months old and legal action is advisable by the time they are three months old. Prepare an overdue accounts list by invoice dates.

Ledger account
Name
Address

Account No

Date	Invoice or Cheque No	Brief Details		DR		CR		BALANCE

Overdue list

No	Name	TOTAL BALANCE	Current	1 month Overdue	2 months Overdue	3 months Overdue	4 months Overdue	5 months Overdue
ACCOUNT			Analysis of balance					

Wages records

When employees are taken on, tax and National Insurance have to be deducted from their wages or salary and paid by the employer to the Inland Revenue in the following month.

Records have to be kept and be available for inspection by the Inland Revenue to see that the laws are obeyed. This means keeping a Wages Book and proper tax deduction cards.

The Wages Book must show how each person's earnings are calculated (regular fixed weekly or monthly amount, or hours worked times hourly rate, overtime, bonus etc) and show all the deductions made to arrive at the net pay put into each pay packet.

Instructions on how to calculate tax and national insurance deductions will be provided by Inland Revenue.

Specialised Wages Books are obtainable inexpensively from most stationers' shops and should be examined. If they are suitable they can save time because forms do not have to be written out and may help in avoiding errors.

Stock records and stock control

Stocks are:

Raw materials from which goods for sale are to be produced
Goods bought for resale but not yet sold
Goods in course of production but not completed
Materials purchased to carry out a job or contract for a customer
Jobs or contracts started but unfinished
Goods produced and awaiting sale
Goods, jobs or contracts completed or sold but not yet invoiced
Office stationery.

All such items are the property or assets of the business until they are used or sold.

Their cost is not part of the cost of goods sold and, therefore, must not be charged to the profit and loss account (ie, deducted from the income from sales) until they are used or sold.

At the close of each accounting period, when a statement of profit and loss is to be prepared, there must be a stock-taking and all stocks must be listed and valued at the lower of their cost or their replacement value.

The total value of such stocks will be deducted from the total value of

Wages

No	Name	Hours worked			Rate per hour	Gross pay	Adj	Tax-able pay	Tax	NI	Other deductions				Total ded	Tax-able pay less ded	Adj	Net pay	Er's NI
		Basic	O/T 1	O/T 2	Total															

WAGES

purchases thus excluding them from the Profit and Loss Account but it will be shown in the Balance Sheet as one of the business assets.

A good plan is to list the stocks in a book to form a permanent record so that each stock-taking can be easily compared with the previous one. An examination can then be carried out to identify stocks which are at a low level and should be increased, or at too high a level so that action should be taken for their reduction, or stocks which are slow-moving or not moving at all and they equally require attention.

Do not allow your money to be locked up in unnecessary stocks – it can be put to better use.

To count stock and value it at the end of each accounting period may be difficult to carry out in practice.

In such an instance the following steps are recommended:

1. Record purchases of stock items in separate analysis columns in the Purchases Book and/or Cash and Bank Books.
2. Analyse cash and credit sales to identify the stock items involved so that their cost can be calculated.
3. Opening stock value, plus purchases, minus sales, equals estimated value of stocks at the end of the period.

Similarly, if manufactured stock is involved, a record of production can be kept to include its cost (which may even be calculated by deducting a known gross profit from the selling value). If sales from manufactured stock are analysed separately and their cost calculated, an estimated value of stock can be assessed as described above, namely opening stock plus cost of manufacture minus cost of items sold equals cost of stock at end of period.

The most common errors in calculating theoretical stocks arise from the failure to identify such things as:

1. Goods which have been received but for which no invoices have been written into the Purchases Book.
2. Goods which have been despatched to customers but have not yet been invoiced.

It is important to adjust the purchases and sales shown in the books to allow for such eventualities.

Such estimated stock values are bound to be inaccurate but with experience they can be acceptable. However, to make sure that they are not too far out, a stock count should be made as often as possible,

Stocks

ITEM	Month			Month			Month		
	Quantity	Price	Cost	Quantity	Price	Cost	Quantity	Price	Cost
Totals									

perhaps every three or six months. Certainly, the accountant will insist on a stock count at the end of each year.

Fixed assets

The following items form part of the business property or assets:

Land
Buildings
Plant and machinery
Tools
Fixtures and fittings
Office furniture and equipment
Vehicles

The cost of purchasing them must not be charged in the Profit and Loss Account for the period during which they are purchased. They usually have a long life. Vehicles may last for five years, machinery for 10 or 20 years, buildings for 50 years or more.

The cost of fixed assets must be spread over their lives.

Assess the likely life of each asset, ie, if a vehicle is expected to last for four years, charge each year's accounts following the purchase with one-quarter of the cost.

Depreciation is:

the proportion of the asset's value which is said to have been used; and

the amount by which the value of the asset has gone down – depreciated – because of its age or because it has been used.

The depreciation is charged against the sales of each year in the Profit and Loss Account.

The 'written down value' – the cost of the asset after deducting the depreciation for each year since its purchase – is included in the Balance Sheet as part of the business assets.

A record should be kept of all fixed assets purchased and every such purchase written into the record as it happens.

The record must show a description of the asset, its cost, its expected life and thus the rate at which it is to be depreciated.

The record should be kept in a permanent book with sufficient analysis columns to allow, in each successive year of the life of each asset, its depreciation and its net written down value.

Register of fixed assets

Date of Purchase	Description of Asset	Exp- ected Life	Cost	Year		Year		Year		Year	
				Dep'n	Net Value	Dep'n	Net Value	Dep'n	Net Value	Dep'n	Net Value
	Total										

Thus each year the total charge for depreciation on all the assets to be charged to Profit and Loss Account and the net written down value of all assets to be written in the Balance Sheet can both be added up.

Assets which are leased, bought on hire-purchase, mortgaged or subject to government grants such as Regional Development Grants, require special treatment and your accountant's advice must be sought for such items.

Your accounts and your accountant

If you have kept good records of your cash transactions which can be traced to your bank statement and each month you have reconciled your bank statement with your bank book in which you have shown monthly totals of receipts from sales and other sources and payments analysed to types of expense, your accountant has only to summarise 12 monthly totals from your bank book to assess the money which you owe and are owed (your 'Bills to pay' and 'Money to collect' files) and attend to the more complex items like hire purchase and lease payments and depreciation.

He can produce for you a Profit and Loss Account and a Balance Sheet.

The Profit and Loss Account is really made up of three elements:

1. Income from sales.
2. Direct costs – such as raw materials or goods purchased for resale – which are incurred only as a direct result of making the sales.
3. Running costs – your fixed expenses like rent, office expenses etc – which are incurred just by being in business and have to be paid whether you make any sales or not.

If direct costs are deducted from income from sales you are left with what is called Gross Profit and if the running costs are deducted from this you are left with *profit before tax*.

Clearly gross profit is a vital item. The prices you pay for raw materials for your production of goods and for goods you buy for resale, the efficiency of your labour and the prices you charge your customers must all be such that the gross profit you are left with is greater than your running costs – if it is not you will make a loss instead of a profit.

The object in business is to keep running costs to a minimum and earn as much profit as you can.

The Balance Sheet is really made up of two elements.

1. A summary of the funding of the business – money invested by personal capital, loans and profit retained over the years.
2. A summary of how the money is invested – a statement of assets and liabilities which represent the worth of the business, ie:

> Stocks of raw materials and stock in trade
> + Debtors, who owe you money
> + Cash in hand and at the bank
> = CURRENT ASSETS
> − Creditors, to whom you owe money
> = NET CURRENT ASSETS
> + Fixed assets (the value of plant, machinery, vehicles, office equipment and buildings)
> = TOTAL ASSETS

Good financial management results in profit becoming money in the bank to finance growth in the business instead of being tied up in stocks which can become redundant or debtors who may not pay up.

Chapter 2

A Closer Look at Accounting

This chapter takes bookkeeping a stage further and ventures into the preparation of management accounts.

Schedule of accounts

To get the best advantage from your accounts it will be necessary to analyse your income and expenditure. For example, although most income will be generated from sales of products or services, you will need to be aware of income which may be from other sources such as occasional sales of assets, government grants, loans, personal funds contributed, sales of shares in the business etc. Expenses must be analysed between their various causes. First, all expenses can be divided between 'Direct', 'Indirect' and 'Fixed' ie:

Direct	Expenses which are directly attributable to the product or service. Such expenses, (like raw materials) would not arise if the product or service was not made.
Indirect	Expenses which may vary according to the volume or level of business. For example, electric power may vary if more machines are switched on or if shift working is undertaken.
Fixed	Expenses which, in the short term at least, do not vary. They are the costs of establishing the business which arise even if there are no sales. Examples are expenses such as rent, rates and insurance.

Second, each of these broad divisions should be further broken down to types of expense like telephones, car expenses, repairs, advertising, etc. In the course of this analysis you could group the expenses according to activities such as 'Selling', 'Production' and 'Administration'.

There is an almost endless number of headings to which income and expenditure can be analysed but remember that the more headings you use the more complicated your bookkeeping will become and the more liable you are to make mistakes.

Therefore decide carefully the extent of analysis you need to control your business effectively. Remember that the purpose of the analysis is to guide you as to where money comes from and goes to. Try to prepare a list of just enough headings to do just that and one that does not swamp you with a mass of detail which may cloud the real issues.

Such a list is illustrated overleaf and on it each heading, or account, has been given a number.

The important thing to remember when preparing accounts and therefore, when compiling your Schedule of Accounts, is to distinguish between 'Capital' and 'Revenue' as regards both receipts and expenditure.

Capital receipts are the amounts subscribed by the proprietor or the partners (or the shareholders in the case of a limited company) and such items as loans to the business and the proceeds from the occasional sales of assets.

Capital expenditure is all expenditure incurred in purchasing assets (like land, buildings, plant or vehicles) required for the purpose of earning income from the business.

Revenue receipts are the amounts received by the business from the sale of its products, goods or services.

Revenue expenditure is all expenditure incurred in carrying on the business and in manufacturing its products, purchasing goods or providing a service (like materials for production, goods for resale, wages, salaries, rent and general overheads). Capital receipts and expenditure are summarised in the Balance Sheet which discloses the value of the business assets and liabilities on a particular date, such as the end of the financial year. Revenue receipts and expenditure are summarised in the Profit and Loss Accounts which discloses the income and thus the profit or loss on the trading of the accounting period such as a month, a quarter, or a year.

Therefore you will see that in the illustrated Schedule of Accounts all the Revenue Accounts have been listed separately from the Capital Accounts which represent assets and liabilities. Also the Revenue Accounts are numbered in such a way as to separate direct, indirect and fixed expenses, ie:

100   Income from Sales
200   Direct costs
300   Indirect costs

Schedule of accounts

	Revenue			Assets and liabilities
101	Sales Product 1		610	Stocks – raw materials
102	2		611	– work in progress
103	3		612	– saleable goods
104	4			
105	5		620	Debtors
106	6		621	Prepayments
109	Sundry sales			
			630	Cash at bank
201	Raw materials		631	Office cash
211	Direct wages and NI			
220	Carriage outwards		701	Creditors
301	Indirect wages and NI		702	Accrued charges
302	Salaries and NI			
			710	HP creditors
401	Consumable stores		715	Grant suspense
402	Repairs		720	Wages creditors (net pay)
403	Power, light and heat		721	PAYE NI
404	Advertising		722	Other deductions from wages
405	Travelling		730	VAT input
406	Entertaining		731	VAT output
407	Printing and stationery		732	Net VAT
408	Postages and telephones		740	Tax
409	Office expenses			
410	Professional charges		801	Land and buildings
411	Sundry		802	Plant and machinery
412	Vehicle running costs		803	Motor vehicles
413	Hire purchase interest		804	Office equipment
414	Bank charges		805	Fixtures and fittings
415	Bank interest			
416	Loan interest		810	Accumulated depreciation
417	Rent and rates			
418	Insurance		901	Share capital
419	Bad Debts		902	Loans
420	Drawings		903	Proprietor's capital
499	Depreciation			
			910	Profit and Loss of previous
501	Sundry income			years
502	Discount received		911	Profit and Loss of current year
503	Discount allowed			

Note: The revenue accounts such as 'raw materials' and 'direct wages' can be extended to show costs per product, as with 'Sales' if required.

The accounts nos. 401 to 420 can be divided into groups corresponding to such activities as 'Administration', 'Selling', etc, if desired.

This list of accounts is not exhaustive, it can be advisable to divide expenses into many more headings but greater analysis means more work, more chance of error and perhaps more complicated accounts which become more difficult to read and understand.

400 Fixed costs
500 Sundry revenue
600 Current assets
700 Liabilities
800 Fixed assets
900 Funds provided and profit earned

Enter the accounts and the numbers in the headings of the analysis columns of the Sales Book and Purchases Book as appropriate and in the Cash and Bank Books. In the Cash and Bank Books only a minimum of headings will be necessary. These will be accounts like: wages; payment of VAT to HM Customs and Excise; and payment of PAYE to Inland Revenue. These are payments which are not made against invoices. Most invoices will be for credit purchases and will be written into the Purchase Book and all cheques in payment of such invoices will, therefore, be analysed to a column headed 'Creditors' in the Bank Book.

Similarly, most receipts may be for sales on credit, the invoices for which will have been written into the Sales Book and the cheques received in settlement of these invoices will be analysed to a column headed 'Debtors' in the Bank Book.

Suggested column headings are shown in the examples but the final decision is yours, based on the accounts you believe the most important to be monitored. The columns headed 'Others' or 'Sundry' will need to be analysed separately at each month end – unless you use an analysis book with many more columns.

By putting the account numbers at the head of each column the job of writing up the Trial Balance will be made easier. To provide extra analysis columns in the Purchases Book it is commonly helpful to divide the book into two books:

1. Raw materials and direct costs.
2. General purchases.

The 'Raw material and direct costs' book can then have plenty of columns to analyse these costs between types of purchases or between products.

It can also be helpful to divide the Sales Book between UK sales and exports or between sales direct to consumers, to retailers and to wholesalers.

Specimen headings of analysis columns

BANK BOOK

Date	Pay-in No	Received from	Total	Debtors 620	Others	Date	Chq No	Paid to	Total	Creditors 701	Net Pay 720	PAYE 721	Other ded'ns 722	Office cash 631	VAT 730	Others	Balance at Bank

PURCHASES BOOK

Date	Inv No	Supplier	Inv Total 301	VAT 730	Net	Date paid	Raw mat'ls 201	Stores 401	Repairs 402	Power 403	Adv 404	Travel 405	Ent'g 406	Print'g 407	Tel 408	Office exp. 409	Prof chge 410	Others

SALES BOOK

Date	Inv No	Customer	Inv Total 620	VAT 731	Net	Date rec'd	P'duct 1 101	2 102	3 103	4 104	5 105	6 106

WAGES & SALARY RECORD

No	Name	Department	Gross Pay 211	Tax PAYE 721	EEB NI 721	Other ded'n 722	Total ded'n	Net pay 720	ERS NI 721

47

Special note re posting of wages and salaries in books.

Assume: Gross pay £100

Deductions – PAYE		25	
Employee's NI		10	
Savings Scheme		5	40
Net pay – actual payment to employee			£60

Note: Employer's NI contribution £10.

In books:

	A/C 211 Gross Pay	A/C 721 PAYE/ NI	A/C 722 Other deductions	A/C 720 Net Pay	A/C 630 Cash at Bank
Pay due (from payroll)*	110	(45)	(5)	(60)	
When wages paid				60	(60)
When Revenue paid		45			(45)
When other deductions paid			5		(5)
Account balances	110	—	—	—	(110)

Preparation of accounts

At the end of each month:

1. Add up all the columns of the principal books – Cash Book, Bank Book, Purchases Book, Sales Book – and make sure that the totals of all the analysis columns add up to the Total column.
2. Check that the total of deposits of cash into the bank shown in the Cash Book agrees with the total of cash paid in as shown in the Bank Book. Similarly check that the amount of cash withdrawn from the bank as shown in the Bank Book is accurately recorded in the Cash Book.
3. Check that the balance of cash in hand shown in the Cash Book actually does exist.
4. Reconcile the Bank Book with the bank statement.
5. If you are using personal ledgers to record transactions with your customers or suppliers they must be reconciled as follows:

   (a) *Customers*. Extract a list of balances owed to you by each individual customer, scrutinise them to make sure that they are accurate. Check that the total of all such balances equals the previous month's total plus the total value of sales invoices issued during the month (including VAT), as shown in the Sales Book minus the total cash received from customers which is the total analysed to the Debtors columns in the Bank and Cash Books. If there is a difference it must be found and corrections made.

   (b) *Suppliers*. Carry out the same exercise as for customers, but of course, using the total purchases (including VAT) shown in the Purchases Book and the cash and cheque receipts analysed to creditors. Also, when scrutinising the balances owed to individual suppliers, check them against any suppliers' statements you have received, query any discrepancies and make adjustments to your books if necessary.

At this stage you will know precisely:

1. How much money you have received and from whom.
2. How much money you have spent and on what.
3. Your cash and bank balances.
4. What you have purchased and to whom you owe money.
5. What you have sold and who owes you money.

For an approximate guide to your state of affairs take the following steps. To the value of your stock of materials (products ready for sale and goods bought for resale), add the amount owed to you and your bank and cash balances, now deduct what you owe, including your bank overdraft if you have one. Then add the value of your fixed assets (buildings, plant and vehicles which you own), including the cost of any assets bought during the period, as shown by your analysis of payments in your Bank Book.

This will tell you the net value of your assets and if this value has increased since you last calculated it, the amount of the increase is roughly the profit you have made. If it has decreased you have made a loss.

This is only an approximate guide and it can be grossly misleading unless you take into account items such as your outstanding debt to Inland Revenue for PAYE deducted from wages paid to employees, your VAT debt to HM Customs and Excise, deposits received from customers in advance of your delivering their goods, payments you have made in advance of the receipt of goods or services, HP or lease payments due etc. Therefore you should take matters further and produce a *trial balance*, if not monthly, at least every three months to make sure you are aware of the true state of affairs.

Things to remember

1. Your Profit and Loss Account, unlike an Income and Expenditure Account, is based upon invoice sales – not cash received – and expenses incurred or invoiced to you and relating to the accounting year or period – not on payments made.
2. The VAT you have charged on your sales invoices is money which does not belong to you. Ultimately you have to pay these amounts over to HM Customs and Excise, but when making the payment you can deduct the VAT which you have paid on the purchases you have made from your suppliers. Therefore VAT is neither a receipt nor an expense as far as your Profit and Loss Account is concerned and it must be excluded. Instead, the amount you owe to HM Customs and Excise must be included with your creditors to whom you owe money.

Prepayments and provisions

When writing up the Balance Sheet and the Profit and Loss Account it is important to review all the accounts to make sure that all sales and purchases are properly included in so far as they relate to the period under review.

Examples

Rent is sometimes payable in advance. It can happen that the most recent rent bill relating say to the quarter ending 31 March will have been entered in the Purchases Book, when it was received during December. Because it is in the Purchases Book, whether it has been paid or not, it will have been analysed to the account No 417 – 'Rent and Rates' and included with the other overheads when summarising the Trial Balance at the end of December. But if accounts are being made up for the period to December this bill does not relate to that period and so it must be excluded.

This is a prepayment – ie, a cost included in one month's figures which relates to a subsequent month or period.

Conversely electricity bills are usually paid in arrears so it is unlikely that the bill for the quarter ended 31 December will have been received in time for inclusion in the December Purchases Book. So this is an expense which has to be added in to the figures. *This is a provision* – ie, an expense which has not been included in the books and must be provided for.

It is necessary to go through all the accounts and check them in this way and in this connection the analysis columns in the books will make it easier to identify the missing charges and those which do not apply to the period.

It is particularly important to verify that all despatches to customers have been invoiced and, if not, provisions must be made to ensure that the value of goods not invoiced is included.

Likewise a check must be made to see that all goods received have been invoiced and the invoices recorded in the Purchases Book. If not, provisions must be made for the cost of these items.

Depreciation is a provision which has to be made each time accounts are prepared. Every asset has an expected life: a vehicle four years, a desk five years, a machine tool ten years and so on. Clearly it would be wrong to include the cost of an asset in the cost of sales for the year in which it was purchased. Its cost should be spread over each of the years of its expected life. Estimate the charge for depreciation for the year from the Fixed Asset Register and enter in the Journal, one-twelfth of the annual amount for each of the months to which your Trial Balance relates.

Include in your estimate the depreciation appropriate to any expenditure on new fixed assets which you intend to purchase during the year.

The way to make the provisions and prepayments in the accounts is to record them in a Journal from which you will enter them on the Trial Balance. You then have a permanent record of the provisions and prepayments you have assessed.

Leasing, lease purchase and hire purchase contracts

The recording of such transactions in the accounts hinges upon whether legal title or ownership of the asset passes eventually to the person who enters into the contract.

In the case of a lease or hire, ownership normally does not pass and therefore the payments to the leasing or hiring company have to be charged against the sales of the business when arriving at the profit. This requires no special bookkeeping treatment. The monthly or quarterly invoices and payments are written into the Purchases Book and Bank Book like any other purchase.

In the case of lease purchase or hire purchase, ownership does pass to a greater or lesser degree and, therefore, a different treatment is required.

In simple terms, the cost of the asset can be expressed as:

Price of asset if bought outright for cash+interest payable
= Total payable to the lease/hire purchase company over the life of the contract.

This transaction is regarded as a normal purchase on credit terms except that the credit terms are extended over a longer period and payment is made in instalments. Usually a deposit is payable which may be equal to three instalments in advance and sometimes the total VAT is payable at the same time as the deposit. Subsequent instalments are payable probably by a standing order which is dealt with by the Bank. Therefore, there may be no invoice, as such, to write into the Purchases Book and no cheques to enter in the Bank Book. Instead, there is a lease/hire purchase agreement which sets out all the particulars.

For example:

	£
Cash Price	8,000
Interest	1,600
Total payable	9,600
in 1 deposit of	960
and 54 instalments of	160

51

Notice that each instalment is made up of:

Capital cost (cash price)	133.33
plus interest	26.67
	£160.00

If the asset had been purchased for cash the following bookkeeping entries would have been made via the Purchase Book and the Bank Book.

On receipt of invoice:

Plant and machinery	Account 802	Dr £8,000.00	
To Creditors	Account 701		Cr £8,000.00

On payment of invoice:

Creditors	Account 701	Dr £8,000.00	
To bank account	Account 630		Cr £8,000.00

In the special circumstances of a lease/hire purchase, the agreement document is used to make a Journal entry to record the acquisition of the asset and the acceptance of a liability to pay a lease/hire purchase creditor as follows:

On signing of agreement:

Plant and machinery	Account 802	Dr £8,000.00	
To lease/HP creditor	Account 710		Cr £8,000.00

The deposit and subsequent instalments must be split between the amounts which repay the lease/hire purchase creditor for the cash price and the amounts of interest payable which is a charge in the Profit and Loss Account.

The deposit is probably payable by cheque and will be recorded in the Bank Book and analysed to a column headed 'Lease/HP payments'. The instalments will be picked up when doing the bank reconciliation and will be put into the Bank Book at this stage and analysed to the column 'Lease/HP payments'. The total of the lease/hire purchase payments column will have to be split between cash price repayments and interest, by making Journal entries as follows:

On payment of deposit

Lease/HP creditor	Account 710	Dr £800.00	
Lease/HP interest	Account 413	Dr £160.00	
To Bank Account	Account 630		Cr £960.00

On payment of each standing order

Lease/HP creditor	Account 710	Dr £133.33	
Lease/HP interest	Account 413	Dr £ 26.67	
To bank account	Account 630		Cr £160.00

If there are several lease/purchase agreements it can be helpful to make up a schedule of the agreements on which each monthly or quarterly payment can be analysed between cash price repayments and interest. It would then be possible to analyse each Standing Order in the Bank Book by analysing it between columns headed 'Lease/HP payments and 'Lease/HP interest'. This would avoid the necessity of making the Journal entries.

By either of these means the interest payable will be shown as a charge against the profits of the business and the Lease/Hire Purchase Creditor liability will be extinguished over the life of the agreement. For so long as the liability remains it will be shown on the Balance Sheet as a 'Creditor – due after more than one year'.

From the outset, the purchase of the asset will be recorded in the fixed asset register and its value taken into account, like that of all the other assets, when calculating the depreciation charge for the year.

Government grants

The treatment of government grants will vary according to the basis of different grant schemes introduced from time to time by successive governments. Grants are sometimes available towards revenue expenditure on such items as research and development of a new product, marketing or installation of financial control systems. Revenue grants may also be received on the basis of job creation. Other grants may be obtainable towards capital expenditure – on the acquisition of a fixed asset.

Revenue grants should be taken into the Profit and Loss Account as income in the same period in which the expenditure to which they relate is incurred, taking care to show such income in a separate account from ordinary trading income.

Capital grants should be credited to 'Fixed Assets' and shown in the Fixed Asset Register as reducing the cost of the assets in question. By this means the depreciation of the asset will be reduced and effectively, the benefit of the grant will be spread over the expected life of the asset. Sometimes there is a liability to repay all or part of the grant if certain conditions are not met. In such cases the grant should be credited to a 'Grant Suspense Account' which will show as a liability in the Balance Sheet. For example, when the cheque for the grant is received and written into the Bank Book, analyse it to a column headed 'Grant Suspense'. The book-keeping entry would be:

Bank account	Account 630 Dr £900.00	
To grant suspense	Account 715	Cr £900.00

Whenever a Trial Balance is prepared, the amount of the liability still outstanding can be assessed and the balance of the Suspense Account reduced accordingly by crediting the expired amount to the appropriate Revenue Account or, in the case of a capital grant, to the Depreciation Account by means of an entry in the Journal. For example, suppose a capital grant of £900 has a condition that the asset must be retained in the business for three years.

At the end of each month the outstanding liability may be said to have reduced by £25 and the Journal entry would be:

Grant suspense	Account 715 Dr £25.00	
To depreciation	Account 499	Cr £25.00

At the end of the three years the Suspense Account will be zero because no further liability exists and the grant will have been absorbed into the Profit and Loss Account.

The Journal

The Journal is used for the correction of errors, for entering prepayments and provisions and for posting the payroll.

Journal entries for correction of errors
Inevitably errors will be made, like amounts analysed to the wrong column in the Purchases Book. Rather than scratch it out and alter the book, the proper way to make the correction is by a Journal entry.

Example

An invoice for electricity has inadvertently been analysed to the column for rent. So the Journal entry is:

Electricity	Account 403	Dr £106.26	
To rent and rates	Account 417		Cr £106.26

Journal entries for prepayments

Prepayments	Account 621	Dr £400.00	
To rent and rates	Account 417		Cr £400.00

Being rent for quarter ending 31 March carried forward to the following quarter.

Journal entries for provisions

Electricity	Account 403	Dr £100.00	
To provisions	Account 702		Cr £100.00

Being the electricity bill estimate for the quarter ended 31 December.

For depreciation

Depreciation	Account 499	Dr £1,000.00	
To accumulated depreciation	Account 810		Cr £1,000.00

Being the charge for depreciation of fixed assets for the quarter ended 31 December.

For the payroll

Direct wages and ERS NI*	Account 211	Dr £1,500.00	
Indirect wages and ERS NI*	Account 301	Dr £ 500.00	
Salaries and ERS NI*	Account 302	Dr £ 500.00	
To PAYE/NI	Account 721		Cr £1,000.00
Other deductions	Account 722		Cr £ 100.00
Net pay	Account 720		Cr £1,400.00
		£2,500.00	£2,500.00

Being details of pay and deductions from the payroll for December.
Note: These amounts include gross earnings and the employers NI contributions.

The Journal ensures a good record of all corrections, prepayments and provisions. Notice that each entry has a short description as a future reminder of the reason for the entry.

Journal

JOURNAL				
Ref No	Account	Account No	DR	CR

The trial balance

This is the document which you will use to prove the mathematical accuracy of your bookkeeping. It is simply a large sheet of analysis paper with twelve analysis columns across it.

List all the accounts from your Schedule of Accounts down the left-hand side of the sheet as illustrated overleaf, listing first the Revenue Accounts and then the Capital Accounts.

Next head-up the columns. The first column must be headed 'Balances brought forward' and in this column you will be writing the balances on all the accounts at the beginning of the accounting period. If it is the first Trial Balance since the start-up of the business the only entries will probably be the bank balance which will be your only asset, balanced by your own capital input and any loans received which make up your capital employed. In accounting terms these are business liabilities because the business is liable to repay such items.

Head the next six columns with the various books and records: Sales; Purchases; Cash; Bank; Wages; and Journal. Then you need a column headed 'Sub-total', the purpose of which will be explained later.

The next three columns should be headed: Stocks; Provisions and Prepayments. The last column is headed 'Closing Balances' and in this you will be writing the total of all the numbers written on each line across the page.

Completing the trial balance

In double entry bookkeeping, every debit entry must have a corresponding credit entry. The invoice total of all the sales invoices sent out during the month and recorded in the Sales Book represents two things:

1. The amount of money owed to you by your customers. Because money owed to you is one of your business assets, it is a capital item and is debited to the Debtors Account and will appear on your Balance Sheet.
2. The value of your sales for the month which is a Revenue item and is credited to the Sales Account which will appear in your Profit and Loss Account.

However, any VAT included on your sales invoices is not income of your
business from sales because that amount does not belong to you but to HM Customs and Excise to whom you will have to account for it on your next VAT quarter date. So only the net total of the month's

Trial balance

	Balances b/fwd	Sales	Purchases	Bank	Fixed Assets	Wages	Journal & Corrections	Sub-total c/fwd	Stocks	Journal Prepay & Provis	Closing Balances
PROFIT & LOSS											
101 Sales		(69,000)						(69,000)			(69,000)
109 Sundry sales		(1,000)						(1,000)			(1,000)
201 Raw materials			47,500					47,500	(2,500)		45,000
211 Direct wages						6,000		6,000			6,000
220 Carriage											
GROSS PROFIT											19,000
302 Salaries						4,000		4,000			4,000
402 Repairs											
403 Power			294				106	400		100	500
404 Adverts											
405 Travelling											
407 Printing			380					380			380
408 Post & Telephones			250					250			250
409 Office expenses			10	70				80			80
410 Professional			300					300			300
412 Vehicle expenses			1,000					1,000			1,000
414 Bank charges				40				40			40
417 Rent & Rates			2,306				(106)	2,200		(400)	1,800
418 Insurance			200					200			200
420 Drawings								6,000			6,000
499 Depreciation										450	450
OVERHEADS			4,740	110		10,000		14,850		150	15,000
PROFIT											4,000

BALANCE SHEET								
610 Stocks – Materials						1,000		1,000
611 WIP						500		500
612 Saleable						1,000		1,000
620 Debtors	3,000	80,500		(73,500)		10,000		10,000
621 Prepayments							400	400
630 Cash	5,000			1,080		6,080		6,080
CURRENT ASSETS								18,980
701 Creditors	(2,000)		(59,840)	57,500	(1,150)	(5,490)		(5,490)
702 Provisions							(100)	(100)
720 Net Pay				12,500	(13,500)	(1,000)		(1,000)
721 PAYE				2,300	(2,500)	(200)		(200)
732 VAT		(10,500)	7,600	10	150	(2,740)		(2,740)
740 Tax								
NET CURRENT ASSETS	6,000							9,450
801/5 Fixed Assets	4,000				1,000	5,000	(450)	4,550
TOTAL ASSETS	10,000							14,000
902 Loans								
903 Prop Capital	8,000					8,000		8,000
910 Profit – prev yrs	2,000					2,000		2,000
911 Profit this year								4,000
CAPITAL EMPLOYED	10,000							14,000

Note: Figures in brackets denote credits.

invoices (excluding VAT) is your revenue and is credited to the Sales Account. But VAT is one of your liabilities which is a capital item that is credited to the VAT Account which will appear on your Balance Sheet.

Now make these entries:

1. In the column headed 'Sales' write the totals from the Sales Book against the appropriate accounts, putting credits in brackets (or in red). You will find that all the credits will add up to the same total as all the debits and that the total of the column is therefore zero. If this is not so you have made an error somewhere and it must be found and corrected.

2. Do the same thing with the Purchases Book, but in this case the invoice total of purchases is money you owe (or perhaps have paid) for your purchases during the period and must be credited to the Creditors Account, whilst the totals of the various analysis columns have to be debited to the corresponding accounts. Again the column must add up to zero.

3. Continue similarly with the Cash and Bank Books.

4. Into the column headed 'Wages' copy the period totals from your Wages Record or Payroll relating to wages and salaries paid to employees. Note that the gross pay plus Employers National Insurance is debited to the Wages and Salaries Account because this is the cost to the business. Deductions made from the gross wages or salaries for PAYE and employees National Insurance are credited to PAYE Account because they are liabilities which you have to meet when you pay over the deductions monthly to the Inland Revenue.

   The net pay is credited to the Net Pay Account because this represents your liability for wages and salaries payable during the period. Some of these wages and salaries will have been paid, but the amount paid will already have been entered from the Cash or Bank Book. The difference between the amount paid and the amount written from the Wages Record will be the 'lying on' pay which arises when wages are paid one week in arrears. The difference must be the net pay due for the last week of the period. It is a liability because it will not yet have been paid out to the employees.

5. Now you must cross-cast all the accounts and put the totals so far in the Sub-total column and make sure that it also adds up to zero.

6. Now from your Stock Record, enter in the Stock column the values you have calculated (or estimated) for raw materials, work in progress (uncompleted orders) and finished goods ready for sale or delivery. These are assets of the business and so the amounts are debited to the Stock Accounts. The total value of all stocks must be

credited to the Raw Materials Account because it represents purchases you have made and not used, or production you have not sold. It will thus be excluded from your cost of sales and not charged against the value of sales in your Profit and Loss Account.

7. Next write in all your Journal entries for provisions and prepayments.

   Debit provisions to the various expense accounts involved, because they refer to purchases made or goods received for which invoices have not yet been received or not been written into the Purchases Book before you added it up for the period.

   The total of all provisions is the amount you are liable to pay in due course and must be credited to the Provisions Account. Prepayments – being amounts you have paid in advance of the receipt of the goods or services concerned – are the opposite of provisions and must be credited to the various expense accounts involved because they do not relate to the current period. The total of all prepayments is debited to the Prepayment Account.

8. Finally cross-cast the sheet again on each line adding the Sub-total, Stocks, Provisions and Prepayment columns together and putting the total in the Closing Balances column which itself will add up to zero.

Debits and credits
Because it is often confusing to recognise whether to debit or credit an account – try to remember a simple rule:

Expenses or assets   = Debits
Receipts or Liabilities = Credits

By adding up the following sub-totals in the Closing Balances column you can produce a Profit and Loss Account and a Balance Sheet.

	Account numbers in the series	gives you
Sales and direct costs	100, 200, 300	Gross profit
Indirect and fixed expenses	400, 500	Overheads
Assets	600	Current assets
Liabilities	700	Liabilities
Fixed Assets	800	Fixed assets
Funds contributed	900	Capital employed

Gross profit minus overheads = Trading profit or loss
Current assets minus liabilities = Net current assets
Net current assets plus fixed assets = Total assets

1. Keep a watch on your gross profit as a percentage of your sales. If it is lower than expected – are your prices too low or your direct costs too high, or have you made an error in stock values or forgotten to invoice a delivery?
2. Keep a watch on your current assets in relation to your liabilities. An ideal ratio is current assets being twice the value of liabilities. If liabilities are greater than current assets, ie you owe more than you are owed, you are in trouble. Can you collect from slow payers or can you delay payment of your creditors until you get things back into balance? You have a cash flow problem. You are going to run out of money – do something about it.
3. If your business is profitable the total assets figure should be increasing.
4. Notice that your profit is added to the capital introduced because you are in fact retaining it in the business as additional capital input. Capital employed always equals total assets. If you make a profit and retain it in the business you ensure an increase in the value of total assets, or in other words, the value of your business.

Closing and opening balance columns
The closing balances at the end of each period become the opening balances for the subsequent period. However, you will readily appreciate that stocks, provisions and prepayments change at the end of each accounting period.

It is recommended that the Sub-total column is the one to copy to the Balances Brought Forward column of the next Trial Balance because:

1. The Sub-total column will then show the total income and expenditure for the year to date.
2. You will need only to insert the stocks, provisions and prepayments as calculated at the date of the Trial Balance.
3. The Closing Balance column will show the Profit and Loss Account for the trading period since the beginning of the financial year and by the time you reach month twelve it will show the results for the year.

The Balance Sheet

The Balance Sheet sets out a list of the various assets of the business – the way in which the capital is employed. The value, or total assets, is the full worth of the business and this is a total which must be watched carefully because it is changes in this value which measure the profit or loss of the business.

The values of the various assets must be carefully monitored to ensure that the investment of the business funds – the employment of capital – is wise and safe.

All of the information required to write up the Balance Sheet is to be found in the Trial Balance which is itself a summary of your accounting books and records.

Study the make-up of net assets

1. If Net Current Assets is a negative value – money owed by the business is more than the value of stocks, money owed to it and money in the bank – the business is insolvent, ie, cannot pay its debts and it may be heading for bankruptcy unless corrective action is taken.
2. It is often necessary to hold stocks in order to sustain production, make sales and meet customers' delivery dates, but the amount held in stock should be kept to a minimum because money locked up in this way reduces the available cash and reduces the profit. Stocks which are slow moving and redundant should be sold off.
3. For the same reason, debtors – money owed to the business – should be kept to a minimum by maintaining strict debt collecting. Every endeavour must be made to keep customers to your terms of payment which should be made abundantly clear before credit is allowed.
4. Money needlessly tied up in stocks or debtors would do more for profit if it were in the bank.
5. Creditors – money owed by the business – must not be allowed to get beyond the stage where suppliers become impatient or annoyed. Try to keep to your suppliers' terms of payment so as to preserve your credit standing. It is dangerous for the value of creditors to exceed that of debtors.
6. Ratios of stocks and debtors as a percentage of sales – and creditors as a percentage of current assets – should compare favourably with those for similar businesses which are usually available.
7. The capital employed (alternatively the total assets) is the amount of money invested in the business and the profit for the year is the

The balance sheet

A & B TRADERS
BALANCE SHEET
as as 31 December 1992

			Notes
Employment of capital			
Stocks Raw materials	1,000		Stocks are valued at the lower of cost and realisable value
Work in progress	500		
Finished goods	1,000	2,500	
Debtors Trade	10,000		Amounts due from customers
Non-trade			
HM Customs	400		VAT recoverable
Prepayments			
Others	80	10,400	
Cash In hand			
At bank	6,000	6,080	
Current assets		18,980	
Deduct:			
Creditors – due within one year			
Trade	5,490		Amounts owed to suppliers
Non-trade	1,000		
Bank overdraft			
Inland Revenue	200		PAYE and Nat Ins deducted from wages
HM Customs	2,740		VAT payable

64

Provisions	100		Amounts owed for goods received but not paid for
Others		9,530	Includes tax due on profits
Lease or HP creditor		9,450	
Net current assets (less liabilities)			
Fixed assets Intangible assets			Goodwill
Tangible assets		4,550	Buildings, plant, vehicles, office equipment valued at cost less amounts written off by depreciation
Investments			Valued at the lower of cost and market value
Total assets (less current liabilities)		14,000	
Deduct:			
Creditor – due after more than one year			As creditors above but payment due after one year
Total assets		£ 14,000	
Capital employed			
Partners'/proprietor's capital		8,000	The original investment in the business
Loans			
Retained profit or			
Partners' current accounts:			Profits retained in business split between partners
Balance brought forward	2,000		
Add: profit for the year	10,000		
	12,000		
Deduct: drawings	6,000	6,000	
TOTAL CAPITAL		£ 14,000	

return on that investment. It is worth remembering that this money could have been invested in many ways other than in the business and some of these might have provided a better return. Ignoring factors like job satisfaction and other non-commercial influences, an investment in a business, because it involves considerably more risk, should provide a higher rate of return.

These business ratios are always important criteria to watch out for and aim for although one probably cannot hope to achieve them in the formative years of trading. Indeed it is frequently difficult for an established concern to achieve them continuously.

In general terms the profit earned by the business is the excess in value of its assets over the capital or funds subscribed or invested in it.

The Profit and Loss Account

Another way of calculating profit is through the Profit and Loss Account which is made up as follows:

Sales	from the Sales Book.
<u>Deduct</u>	
Raw materials used	Purchases (from the Purchases Book) plus stock at beginning of period minus stock at the end
Wages	from the Bank Book
<u>Equals</u>	
Gross profit	
<u>Deduct</u>	
Overheads	from the Purchases Book
Depreciation	from the Fixed Asset Record
<u>Equals</u>	
Profit	

The details are obtained from the same books and records as used previously for the Balance Sheet and the profit figure for any given period will, of course, be the same whether calculated by the Profit and Loss Account or the Balance Sheet.

The profit and loss account

A & B TRADERS
Profit and Loss Account
for the year ended 31 December 1992

		Notes
INVOICED SALES	70,000	Excluding VAT
Raw materials used and purchases	45,000	Excluding VAT
Direct wages	6,000	
GROSS PROFIT	19,000	
Staff costs – wages and salaries	4,000	
Overheads	4,550	
Depreciation	450	
TRADING PROFIT	10,000	
Other income	–	Discounts and income from investments
PROFIT or (LOSS)	10,000	
Extraordinary income	–	Items of special non-repetitive nature not related to current year's results
Extraordinary charges	–	
PROFIT or (LOSS) after extraordinary items £	10,000	

NOTE:

1. Salaries and drawings of proprietor or partners are not included as a cost in the Profit and Loss Account because they are, in fact, part of the business profits drawn out in advance.

2. In partnerships, the profit is divided between the partners in the proportion they have agreed and any surplus remaining after deducting their salary and drawings is credited to their respective current accounts.

3. In the case of a sole trader, the profit remaining after deduction of drawings will be credited to his current account or to a retained profit account.

4. The accounts of Limited Companies must be prepared according to Section 228 and Schedule 4 of the Companies Act 1985.

The advantages of the Profit and Loss Account Approach

1. By relating such items as raw materials, wages and gross profit as a percentage of sales, a judgement can be made as to the levels of efficiency and productivity in the business and the correctness of the way you price your sales to customers. For every type of business there is a generally recognised relationship of these items which can be used as targets against which to assess individual performances.
2. It is possible to see whether corrective action is needed to maximise profit – when, for example, the percentage of raw materials or wages to sales is too high, thus making the percentage of gross profit too low.
3. The level of overhead costs can be examined for excessive spending on individual types of expense – travelling, telephones, etc – or in total when perhaps too much of the gross profit is being absorbed by costs leaving too little as profit.

Source and application of funds

It is very important to be aware of the sources from which funds have been introduced into the business and the way in which they have been used.

You will recognise that the Trial Balance starts with the Balance Sheet at the beginning of the period and, by adding to that Balance Sheet all the transactions recorded in the accounting books and records, concludes with a Profit and Loss Account and a Balance Sheet as at the end of the period.

The Statement of Source and Application of Funds summarises the changes in the Balance Sheet brought about by the trading in the period. It shows, for example, whether the profit has been sufficient to finance the working capital requirements or the purchase of assets, or whether it has been necessary to resort to loans or the input of additional funds by the proprietor or partners. It draws attention to the application of funds – the way in which the money has been used – and shows, for example, whether the profit has been withdrawn by the partners, invested in assets or working capital or has resulted in an increase in the bank balance.

A good objective is to make the business self-financing, which is to say that it makes enough profit to meet all its financial needs. Quite often, the generation of profit may be inadequate to meet the cost of modernising plant to remain competitive or to supply the working

Source and application of funds

A & B TRADERS
Source and Application of Funds
for the year ended 31 December 1992

SOURCE OF FUNDS

From trading		
Profit (Loss)		10,000
Adjustment for items not involving the movement of funds.		
Depreciation		450
		10,450
From other sources		
Capital introduced	—	
Sales of fixed assets	—	
Grants	—	
Loans	—	—
TOTAL FUNDS GENERATED		£10,450

APPLICATION OF FUNDS

Purchase of fixed assets	1,000	
Repayment of loans	—	
Drawings	6,000	7,000
Increase (decrease) in working capital:		
Stocks	2,500	
Debtors and prepayments	7,400	
Creditors and provisions	(7,530)	2,370
MOVEMENT IN LIQUID FUND		9,370
Increase (decrease) in cash and bank balances		1,080
		£10,450

capital required for a growth in sales and additional funds have to be injected. It is vital to ensure that these funds are wisely applied so that an acceptable return is made on their investment and that interest on and ultimate repayment of any loans involved can be accommodated. A happy situation exists when profit from trading supplies all the funds required and also increases the bank balance.

Chapter 3
The Nature of Profit

A business never stands still

If it is not growing it is getting smaller and in which case personal drawings are likely to suffer. There needs to be growth, at least enough growth to sustain personal drawings.

But growth, however small, costs money. Cash resources are needed to purchase additional plant or equipment; to replace that which has become obsolete, worn out or outmoded, or simply to increase productive capacity; and to finance the increase in working capital brought about by increased sales.

This money should come from profit. The purpose of profit is to supply finance for the business. It is the savings of the business and, like personal savings, is essential to maintain livelihood. It may not provide all the finance needed so that borrowings may be required. However, few lenders will lend to a business which does not have a profitable track record. Lenders wish to see the business itself supplying some of the finance and taking some of the risk and, more particularly, need to see profitability as evidence that the business can afford to pay interest when due and ultimately repay its borrowings.

How much profit?
The ideal is probably that the profit provides sufficient funds to finance the business without resort to borrowings. However, it may be remembered that the money invested and employed in the business – in buildings, plant, equipment, vehicles and working capital – could have been yielding interest of perhaps 5 per cent or more if placed on deposit with a bank, a building society or in National Savings. Therefore, as a reward for taking a business risk, which may result even in a total loss of the money invested, the business should provide a return of 10 per cent or more per annum. A situation could arise whereby, if the business venture were to earn less than the current bank lending rate, one should invest one's money elsewhere and finance the venture by borrowing.

Working capital

Working capital is most understandably defined as:

Cash (or liquid resources) deployed as:

Stocks	Raw materials needed to sustain production, work in progress or finished production and goods purchased and awaiting sale or delivery to customers.
Debtors	The value of goods delivered and invoiced to customers, but for which payment is awaited, perhaps on credit terms of 7, 30, 60 or even 90 days or more.
Cash	To pay wages and on-going expenses whilst awaiting the receipt of funds from sales or debtors.

Working capital is an element of business financing which is often underestimated. Failure to appreciate its extent is the most common cause of business failure – even in large businesses. Cash flow problems, frequently referred to as if they were an act of God, are usually caused by bad management failing to recognise the full extent of working capital requirements.

Stocks

The purchase of stock, whether as materials for production of goods, or the speculative production or purchase of goods for sale, whilst an essential to making sales and deliveries, is a high risk. A wrong judgement of demand from customers can result in considerable sums of money being locked up in slow moving stock which may even become obsolete and have to be turned into cash at 'knock-down' prices.

Except, perhaps, when you can rely upon a definite price inflation, do not accumulate stocks, even at cheap prices, because the interest which could have been earned on the money so spent will, in all probability, negate most of the apparent savings. Indeed if such stock has to be held for a year before sale, it could well result in a loss if interest is taken into account.

A sound policy is 'Just in time' which means buying or making stock just in time to effect satisfactory delivery to a customer. This entails keeping a careful watch on the suppliers' delivery dates and the speed with which customers require delivery from the placing of their order. In most manufacturing business, the total value of stocks (raw materials, work in progress and finished stock) should not exceed 10–15 per cent of annual sales. In other words stock should be turned over

6–10 times a year. In trading business, involving just buying and reselling, the turnover rate should be much greater.

Debtors

If credit terms of 30 days are offered to customers, goods invoiced between say 1 and 31 January will become payable on 28 February – an average of six weeks after invoicing. But customers' cheques spend 7–10 days in the post or in the bank clearing system and additionally most customers will write their cheques 10–14 days after the due date. Thus, effectively 30 days' credit becomes at best 40 days' and on average 63 days'. As sales grow, the amount owed by customers grows almost in direct proportion.

To provide the goods or services invoiced to customers the business has had to spend money which becomes owed to it. Furthermore, during the 40–63 days whilst waiting for the money to be paid, the business will require more money to continue operating and paying wages and expenses and the burden can be considerable when sales grow quickly or if a big contract is secured.

For this reason terms of payment must be carefully examined so that the resources of the business are not over-strained. It is wise to ask for a deposit with the order and for stage payments at recognisable intervals during a contract which may extend over a period of time, leaving perhaps only a small proportion of the full value of the contract on credit terms following completion. Such arrangements are customary in the construction trades and not uncommon in many others.

The original working capital at the commencement of the business, will have to be provided by cash introduced by the proprietor, by the partners or by loans. Any increase to cope with the growth in sales should be provided by cash generated from profitable trading. Otherwise further funds will need to be introduced by the partners or by further loans.

Example of A & B Traders first year financing

Movements in bank balance and the value of other assets of the business

	(1) Cash at bank £	(2) Debtors £	(3) Stock in trade £	(4) Trading account £	(5) Proprietors capital £
Funds introduced by proprietor at the beginning	5,000				(5,000)
After 3 months' trading					
Sales invoiced				(6,000)	
Cash received from invoices issued in month 1	2,000				
Invoices issued in months 2 and 3 unpaid		4,000			
Amounts paid in cash					
Purchases, including £500 for stock in trade	(4,100)		500	3,600	
Wages of employees	(500)			500	
Expenses	(500)			500	
Own drawings	(1,500)			1,500	
Profit (loss) added to (deducted from) capital				(100)	100
	400	4,000	500		(4,900)

Note: The proprietor has lost £100 of his capital which now stands at £4,900 and is represented by only £400 in the bank, £4,000 owed to him by his customers (debtors) and £500 of goods in stock.

During next 3 months' trading					
Sales invoiced increased by £300 to				(6,300)	
Cash received from invoices issued in months 2 and 3	4,000	(4,000)			
and month 4	2,100				
Invoices issued in months 5 and 6 still unpaid		4,200			
Amounts paid in cash					
Purchases	(3,780)			3,780	
Wages, expenses and drawings	(2,500)			2,500	
Profit, added to capital				20	(20)
	220	4,200	500		(4,920)

Note: The company is now trading profitably but bank balance goes down because more money is owed by customers.

	(1) Cash at bank £	(2) Debtors £	(3) Stock in trade £	(4) Trading account £	(5) Proprietors capital £
During next 3 months' trading					
Invoiced sales again increase by £1,200 to				(7,500)	
Cash received from invoices issued in months 5 and 6	4,200	(4,200)			
and month 7	2,500				
Invoices issued in months 8 and 9 are outstanding		5,000			
Amounts paid in cash Purchases	(4,500)			4,500	
Wages, expenses and drawings	(2,500)			2,500	
Profit, added to capital				500	(500)
	(80)	5,000	500		(5,420)

Note: Although now trading quite profitably and capital now standing at £5,420, the profit has been absorbed by money owed to the business due to upsurge in sales and the bank balance is in overdraft.

	(1) Cash at bank £	(2) Debtors £	(3) Stock in trade £	(4) Trading account £	(5) Proprietors capital £
During the final quarter of year					
Sales invoices increased to				(8,100)	
Cash received from invoices raised in months 8 and 9	5,000	(5,000)			
and month 10	2,700				
Invoices raised in months 11 and 12 still unpaid		5,400			
Amounts paid in cash purchases	(4,860)			4,860	
Wages, expenses and drawings	(2,500)			2,500	
Profit added to capital				740	(740)
	260	5,400	500		(6,160)

Note: Money has started to come back into the bank because the profit is greater than the increase in debtors.

Notice that Profit is the increase in the value of the business and does not necessarily mean more money in the bank. In the example the business was under capitalised – the proprietor needed to have started with more than £5,000, perhaps £6,000, to avoid running out of money.

Although in the year there was a profit of £1,160 at the end there was only £260 in the bank.

The embarrassment of running out of money could have been avoided by the proprietor drawing less, but his standard of living would suffer. Alternatively he might have obtained credit from his suppliers instead of paying cash on delivery. If after six months' trading he had obtained monthly credit terms from his suppliers his payments in cash during the third quarter could have been £1,500 less leaving him with £1,420 in the bank after nine months instead of an overdraft of £80. By the end of the year his bank balance would have been £1,890 instead of £260. Obtaining credit from suppliers is a way of injecting cash into the business as an alternative to subscribing one's own funds or bank or other borrowings, either of which involves interest payments which reduce profits.

In the example the Balance Sheet of the business at its commencement was as shown in column 1 and at the end of the first year was as shown in column 2, but with credit from suppliers it could have been as in column 3.

	(1) £		(2) £		(3) £
Stock	—		500		500
Debtors	—		5,400		5,400
Cash at bank	5,000		260		1,890
Current assets	5,000		6,160		7,790
Deduct					
Creditors	—		—		1,630
Total assets	5,000		6,160		6,160
Proprietor's capital	5,000		5,000		5,000
Add: profit		7,160		7,160	
Deduct: drawings		6,000	1,160	6,000	1,160
Total capital	5,000		6,160		6,160

Note that the profit of a sole trader or partnership is struck before charging drawings which are in fact profits drawn out from the business. It is this profit before deduction of drawings upon which the proprietor is liable to pay income tax. Notice particularly that, in this example, the shortage of money in the bank was caused by the quite rapid increase in sales made on credit terms. A classic example of 'over-trading' or 'cash flow problems' could have been avoided by better financial management or forethought, ie, by obtaining credit from suppliers or negotiating more prompt payment by customers.

Curiously, the cash problem would not have arisen if sales had grown less rapidly, but then, the profit would have been less so this would be a negative attitude. Even so, it is one which may have to be adopted when finance or terms of payment cannot be agreed to support a rapid growth.

In any month, an increase in sales on credit terms, increases the debtors (money owed to the business) by the amount of the increase. Normally extra direct costs arising from the increase in sales have to be paid before money is received from the sales. They have to be met, or financed, from cash in the bank or from cash being generated from other sales.

Imagine a business enjoying a constant income from sales and trading profitably. By keeping its stock holding level its monthly profit of £175 become cash in the bank and accumulates each month.

	End of month 1 £	month 2 £	month 3 £	month 4 £
Starting with a bank balance of £200	375	550	725	900

Now assume that an additional order is to be delivered and invoiced in month 2 for which purchases of stock have to be made and paid for in month 1.

A. *Additional order sales value £500*

	month 1	month 2	month 3	month 4
Purchases of stock in month 1	300			
Cash received from customers in month 4				500
New cash balance	75	250	425	1,100

OR

B. *Additional order sales value £1,000*

	month 1	month 2	month 3	month 4
Purchases of stock in month 1	600			
Cash received from customers in month 4				1,000
New cash balance	−225	−50	125	1,300

77

Observe how in example A the costs of the order can be accommodated by cash-in-hand and cash generated by other sales in month 1. But in example B this is not so and there is a cash flow problem.

Before accepting such an order as in example B:

1. Agree credit terms with supplier so that £600 is not payable until month 2 and obtain, say, 10 per cent deposit from customer either with the order or before delivery.
2. Obtain deposit of 30 per cent with customer's order and the remaining 70 per cent to be paid on credit of 30 days or even 60 days.
3. Arrange an overdraft facility with the bank – but this will involve interest.

Essentially the order does not make a profit until the gross profit (value of sale minus the direct costs) materialises and this does not happen until the customer pays.

Therefore the ideal situation exists when the terms of trading are such that money is received from customers before suppliers have to be paid. Such a situation exists only when personal services are sold for cash on delivery, when goods bought for resale are sold in the same month without having been held in stock awaiting sale or when credit terms allowed by suppliers are as good as or better than those granted to customers. Even retailers who appear to do a 'cash on delivery' trade may have to carry goods in stock in their shop for some while before a customer for them is found.

Be most careful to assess the need for working capital because failure to do so is probably the biggest single cause of business failure.

Selling prices must be adequate to provide a gross profit which exceeds standing costs by a suffficient margin to provide enough profit to supply working capital needs as well as funds for the replacement of assets as they wear out, become obsolete or inadequate for the level of business.

Chapter 4

Profit and Pricing

Gross profit, direct cost and standing cost

Profit is: The excess of income and money receivable over expenditure incurred or committed. In this context, expenditure includes the personal drawings of a sole proprietor or partners.

                The increase in the value of the business – the net value of all its assets less its liabilities – as between one date and another.

Price is: What a purchaser will pay (the price of an article or service is determined by the purchaser not its cost).

                What a seller will accept in return for supplying an article or service.

                A mutual agreement between a willing buyer and a willing seller.

Business income and, therefore, the price of an article or service, has to offset various types of business costs:

Direct costs:

Those directly attributable to the product or service that would not have arisen if the product or service had not been provided. Some wages may be included if their payment is a direct consequence of a particular sale.

Standing costs:

Wages paid to employees to maintain the ability of the business to offer goods or services for sale.

Overhead expenses such as rent, rates, insurances, telephone, stationery, etc that arise even if no sales are made. They are the expenses of maintaining the business establishment. They are fixed and tend not to vary with the level or volume of business.

Personal drawings of the proprietor or partners which are essentially the reason for the existence of the business.

DIRECT COSTS	DIRECT COSTS
STANDING COSTS	GROSS PROFIT
NET PROFIT	

Net Trading Profit:

which remains after all the costs have been met.

Note: Price−direct costs = Gross profit
Gross profit−Standing costs = Net profit

Every article or service has a direct cost associated with it, ie:

the raw materials a manufacturer uses to make his product;
the cost of the product bought by a retailer for resale to his customers;
the cost of replacement parts used by a service contractor when servicing industrial or household equipment;
the cost of paper and paint used by a decorator;
the cost of timber, bricks and cement etc, used by a builder;
the travelling and out-of-pocket expenses of a consultant;
the fuel used by a taxi driver.

The percentage of the price absorbed by direct costs can vary greatly as between different products or services, but always they can be measured and valued quite precisely. Many trades have by custom and practice established a 'norm' for the percentage of direct costs to price, or in the case of retailers, more commonly perhaps, a 'norm' for the mark-up on cost. Often the price of an article or service is also established as a 'going rate' or it can be identified by market research.

	Typical of a manufacturer	*Typical of a retailer*
Price	100	100
Direct cost	60	66.66
Gross Profit margin	40	33.33
Mark-up, Gross Profit to Direct Cost		50

The three fundamental elements which govern the economics of every business are:

direct costs;
gross profit margin
standing costs

These elements apply equally from the sole proprietor to the large international conglomerate.

It is fundamental that the relationship between these three elements is fully understood.

It is the function of the business to discover how to maximise the gross profit within the price available and how to keep standing charges less than the gross profit.

If it were assumed that both the manufacturer and the retailer had standing costs of £10,000 per annum, it is simple to calculate the annual sales which each would require in order to make a profit.

Gross profit margin has to be more than standing costs. Therefore:

If gross profit as
percentage of sales = 40   or   = 33.33
and standing costs = £10,000   = £10,000

sales must be:
$$\frac{10,000 \times 100}{40} \qquad \frac{10,000 \times 100}{33.33}$$
$$= £25,000 \qquad\qquad = £30,000$$

£25,000 or £30,000 is thus the level of sales at which this manufacturer or retailer, respectively, would 'break-even'. Which is to say, would just recover their standing costs and make neither profit nor loss.

It is vital that standing costs are kept as low as possible. There must be no unnecessary faults in the cost structure, otherwise the task of making a profit is made unnecessarily difficult.

Break-even

The break-even Chart 1 shows that an average mark up of 50 per cent on cost (or gross profit of 33⅓ per cent on sales) the gross profit accumulates as sales accumulate until it equals the standing cost when sales reach £30,000. Up to this point – the break-even point – the business is making a loss.

Profit is not earned until sales progress beyond the break-even point. So it is misleading and indeed foolish to calculate prices by adding a percentage for profit to the calculated cost of a job or an article thus, perhaps, believing that each article or job makes a profit.

Pricing does not work that way.

Look at Chart 2
Reducing selling prices by 10 per cent has reduced the mark-up from 50 to 35 per cent on cost. The break-even point has moved up to sales of nearly £40,000. To maintain the level of gross profit and thus the level of trading profit, sales must increase in volume by 43 per cent (ie sales in chart 2 must be increased by 43 per cent from £135 to £193 for a mark up of 35 per cent to give a gross profit of £50 as in Chart 1).

Now look at Chart 3
Increasing prices by 10 per cent, instead of reducing them, raises the mark to 65 per cent on cost and break-even can be reached with sales of only £25,000 with the result that gross profit and trading profit can be maintained even if sales fall by 23 per cent (ie sales in Chart 3 can reduce by 23 per cent from £165 to £127 because even then a mark-up of 65 per cent will give a gross profit of £50 as in chart 1).

Several important things to remember
1. Profit is not earned until sales pass the break-even point.
2. Always be conscious of the break-even point of the business, ie standing cost divided by gross profit margin percentages.

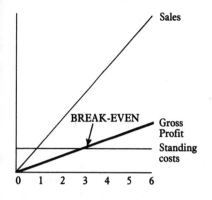

CHART 1

Sales	150
Direct cost	100
Gross Profit	50
Standing cost	10
Profit	40

CHART 2

Sales	135
Direct cost	100
Gross Profit	35
Standing cost	10
Profit	25

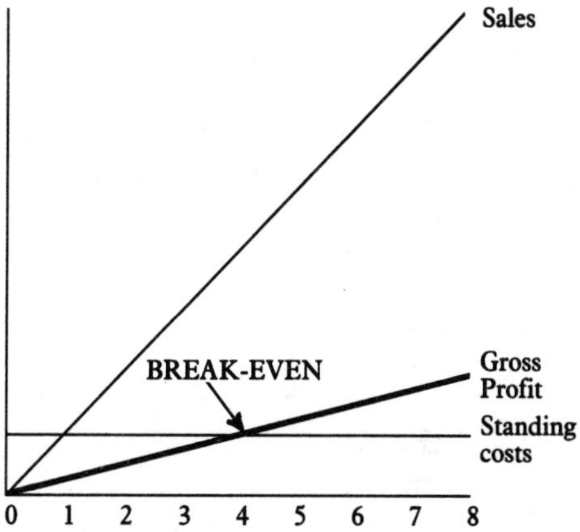

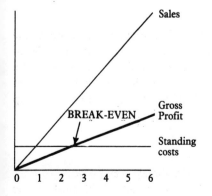

CHART 3

Sales	165
Direct cost	100
Gross Profit	65
Standing cost	10
Profit	55

83

3. Assess the profit potential on each article by its affect on the average gross profit percentage.
4. High gross profit or mark-up percentage means low break-even and low investment in stock and direct costs.
5. Low gross profit or mark-up percentage, more sales required and more expense in stocks and direct costs.

Mix of sales

The business will probably deal in many products or services, each with a different gross profit margin or mark-up. The retailer in the earlier example, having decided that his sales could exceed £30,000 may decide to add 50 per cent to the purchase price of all his stock items to arrive at his selling prices. A simple answer – but what if each item will not sell at 50 per cent mark-up?

Suppose there to be an equal spread of articles bearing mark-up percentages of 30–70 per cent.

Table 1 shows that he can still break-even at sales of £30,000 because the average mark up remains at 50 per cent. But suppose article 5 will not sell, but more of article 3 can be sold.

Table 2 shows that he will have to sell £14,400 of article 3 to make up for the loss on article 5 and to break even his sales must be £31,600 because the average margin has fallen to 46.3 per cent.

Table 3 shows how he could be better off by discontinuing article 1 and promoting the sales of article 4. The average mark up could then be 53.3 per cent and break even at £28,700.

Get the mix of articles sold into the most profitable balance which the market will allow.

Do not cut prices in the hope of attracting more sales. A 10 per cent cut may need more than 30 per cent increase in sales to be of advantage – it seldom works. Cut prices only when you can persuade your supplier to reduce his prices to you.

Estimates and quotations

Standing costs as a cost per hour
In manufacturing and in many other situations, the acceptability of a gross profit margin has to be assessed by comparing it with the standing costs applicable to the product or job in question. When there is no

Table 1

Article	Mark-up %	Buying-in cost	Total mark-up	Sales value
1	30	4.0	1.2	5.2
2	40	4.0	1.6	5.6
3	50	4.0	2.0	6.0
4	60	4.0	2.4	6.4
5	70	4.0	2.8	6.8
		20.0	10.0	30.0

Average mark-up 50 per cent

Table 2

Article	Mark-up %	Buying-in cost	Total mark-up	Sales value
1	30	4.0	1.2	5.2
2	40	4.0	1.6	5.6
3	50	9.6	4.8	14.4
4	60	4.0	2.4	6.4
5	70	—	—	—
		21.6	10.0	31.6

Average mark-up 46.3 per cent

Table 3

Article	Mark-up %	Buying-in cost	Total mark-up	Sales value
1	30	—	—	—
2	40	4.0	1.6	5.6
3	50	4.0	2.0	6.0
4	60	10.7	6.4	17.1
5	70	—	—	—
		18.7	10.0	28.7

Average mark-up 53.5 per cent

known 'going rate' for a particular product or job the best way of ascertaining the price to charge is:

(a) calculate direct cost;

(b) add a gross profit based upon the work hours required to do the work valued at the charge-out hourly rate for standing costs.

The hourly rate for standing costs should be the rate based on the number of hours of work required for the business to break even. The example demonstrates how this hourly cost rate should be calculated.

In many manufacturing businesses it may be necessary to calculate cost rates for various departments, or processes, each of which may not be involved for all items of production, as shown in the following example.

A textile factory may have three departments:

Department 1 – Cutting
Department 2 – Machining
Department 3 – Packing and Despatch

When calculating department or process hourly rates include only the running costs applicable to the department and assess separately the possible and reasonable operating hours in each department. It should be anticipated if some machines in some departments may inevitably remain idle for longer periods of time than others.

For all standing costs, such as administration expenses, which are not distributable to a specific operation, calculate a general rate based upon the overall activity of the business. The gross profit will then be assessed by adding together the separate hours of each department (or cost centre) multiplied by their own hourly cost rate.

Charge-out rate

To calculate charge-out rate
1. List all standing costs and estimate their annual cost (including personal drawings).
2. A year has 52 weeks, but allowing for public and bank holidays, annual holidays etc, there are probably only 47½ working weeks.

Standing cost per week = Annual cost ÷ 47½

3. A 5 day week has 40 hours but allowing for time lost – stoppages, making samples, trials, selling etc, there are probably only 35 possible working hours and the average work-load and efficiency will result in only 85 per cent of these hours being chargeable to customers.

Therefore: hourly cost rate = Standing cost per week ÷ 30

Example of department charge-out rates in a textile factory/department

	Cutting	Machining	Inspection & Packing	TOTAL
Number employed	2	12	3	
Man-hours per week	80	480	120	
Expected utilisation %	60	75	75	
hours	48	360	90	498
A. Break-even at 80% =	38.4	288	70	398.4

	Cutting	Machining	Inspection & Packing	General Admin
Standing costs per week				
Wages	160	960	225	
Overheads directly to department – ie depreciation, power, repairs etc	20	360	40	180
Other costs not directly attributable – ie; rent, telephones, office wages etc	–	–	–	1,000
B. TOTAL	180	1,320	265	1,180
Charge-out rate (B÷A) per hour	4.7	4.6	3.8	3.0

Example of costing for an article

Operation	Minutes required	Charge-out rate per hr £	Standing cost per article (pence)
Cutting	4.0	4.7	31.5
Machining	4.5	4.6	34.5
Inspection	4.0	3.8	25.1
			91.1
General	12.5	3.0	62.4
			153.5
Standing cost			153.5
Direct cost			36.5
Price			190.0

4. The business should make a profit if 30 hours of work are charged out per week.

So it must break even when less than 30 hours are charged out.

It will probably take some 15–20 per cent of the hours charged out to provide a satisfactory profit return on the capital employed.

Therefore: Hourly charge-out rate = Hourly cost rate÷0.80

5. Example

Assume: capital employed = £14,250

standing costs = £11,400

Thus: standing cost per week £11,400÷47½ = £240

hourly cost rate 240÷30 = £8

charge-out rate 8÷0.80 = £10

Hours charged out	Charged out at £10 per hour	Profit
24	£240	Nil
30	300	£60

The required profit of 15 per cent on £14,250 = £2,137 = £45 per week.

This would be achieved when 28½ hours have been charged out in a week.

The benefits of using the charge-out rate can be seen from the tables.

Table 4

A business completing four jobs in a week achieved break-even. If it had completed five jobs it would have made a profit. The fifth job would have made the profit by taking the business beyond its break-even point.

Table 5

Compares the effect of using a charge-out rate instead of using a cost rate and adding a percentage of profit. The percentage profit included in each price was an illusion because in reality the business would have made a loss.

By using the charge out rate:

1. The business can be more certain of breaking even.
2. Selling prices are not so influenced by variations in direct costs.
3. Profit becomes more dependent upon productivity and cost control within the business.

Table 4

Job	Estimate of hours on job	Gross profit added at £10 per hour	Estimate hours on job	Gross profit added at £10 per hour
1	1.75	17.50	1.75	17.50
2	2.00	20.00	2.00	20.00
3	8.25	82.50	8.25	82.50
4	12.00	120.00	12.00	120.00
5	—	—	4.50	45.00
Total	24.00	240.00	28.50	285.00
Cost		240.00		240.00
Profit		Nil		45.00

Table 5

Job	Direct Cost	Gross profit at charge-out rate of £10 per hr	Price	Standing cost at hourly rate £8 per hr	Total cost	Profit at 5% on cost	Price
1	21.00	17.50	38.50	14.00	35.00	1.75	36.75
2	60.00	20.00	80.00	16.00	76.00	3.80	79.80
3	170.00	82.50	252.50	66.00	236.00	11.80	247.50
4	229.00	120.00	349.00	96.00	325.00	16.25	341.25
Total	480.00	240.00	720.00	192.00	672.00	33.60	705.60
Cost	480.00	240.00	720.00				720.00
Profit			Nil				(14.40)

Competition

Having quoted a price to a customer – suppose he will not accept it.

1. Recheck the price calculations.
2. Reduce direct costs by cheaper purchasing.
3. Reduce gross profit required if job can be done in less time.
4. Reduce the charge-out rate.

But consider effect on break-even.

If reducing the quoted price would raise break-even unacceptably, withdraw and look for other customers.

Examples

An article has a direct cost of £21 and takes 1.75 hours to make. Required gross profit 1.75×£10 = £17.50 and price £38.50.

> Customer will only pay £36.
> Can direct costs be reduced to £18.50?
> £36 allows gross profit of £15 so can job be done in 1.50 hours?

> or:

> if already trading above the break-even with a full order book and time to spare;
> all gross profit becomes net profit because standing costs already covered;
> therefore price can be cut.

> But note that such a price is only repeatable under the same trading conditions.

Cutting prices reduces gross profit and raises break-even and could lead to attracting too much cut-price work raising the break-even to a point which would make a profit impossible without greater productivity or reduced direct or standing costs.

The ultimate aim

To make total gross profit for the year exceed standing costs!

Any price for a job which is greater than that job's direct cost makes some contribution to annual gross profit.

Hence: price reductions, special offers, 'sales' by retailers etc can help – especially if they sell off spare working capacity otherwise idle. But they must be seen to be unrepeatable.

Examples

	Sales	Direct cost	Gross profit (thousand £s)	Standing costs	Profit (loss)
Assume expectation to be	36.0	24.0	12.0	10.0	2.0
A. Sales averaging 24.0 and break-even of 30.0 not likely to be reached:					
Sales at normal prices	24.0	16.0	8.0	10.0	(2.0)
Additional sales at 10% price reduction	12.0	9.0	3.0	—	3.0
Annual total	36.0	25.0	11.0	10.0	1.0

	Sales	Direct cost	Gross profit	Standing costs	Profit (loss)
			(thousand £s)		
B. Sales averaging 27.0 and not rising					
Sales at normal prices	27.0	18.0	9.0	10.0	(1.0)
Additional sales at 20% price reduction	9.0	7.5	1.5	—	1.5
Annual total	36.0	25.5	10.5	10.0	0.5
C. Sales at break-even and not rising					
Sales at normal prices	30.0	20.0	10.0	10.0	0.0
Further sales, even at 20% reduction	6.0	5.0	1.0	—	1.0
Annual total	36.0	25.0	11.0	10.0	1.0

Business is a juggling act:
    know what customers will buy;
    match prices to demand;
    secure maximum gross profit;
    keep costs below gross profit.

The bookkeeping must constantly monitor:

    direct costs;
    gross profit;
    standing costs.

Chapter 5
Finance

The business plan

Whether the start up of a new business venture, an expansion project, or any other development of the business involving significant investment, *prepare a business plan* in which is detailed precisely and comprehensively:

The idea and it's future or further development possibilities.
the market and research undertaken;
the marketing plan;
pricing policy;
production methods or purchasing plan;
the sourcing of items of direct cost;
the sourcing of capital assets;
the estimated running costs based upon the envisaged establishment;
a projection of ultimate Profit and Loss Accounts.

Think carefully through the proposal from all angles.

Try particularly to imagine all the arguments against it and avoid being lulled into a feeling of euphoria. Test especially the existence of a market of sufficient volume in which there is room for another supplier at prices which are economically viable. Most instances of apparent opportunities, from bus services in rural areas to travelling shops, are not fulfilled because they are not economically viable.

Distinguish between earning a living in the short term and establish a business which will pay its way for a lifetime and perhaps thereafter.

Whenever possible, find a way of entering a market with a product or service which is different or better than anything existing. Be wary about entering a market with a product or service which is cheaper than those existing – the business could be highly vulnerable to competition. It is better, on balance, to offer quality and a different approach. Customers will pay for quality of product and service at premium prices.

Having thoroughly examined the proposal move on to test how much finance is needed to establish the business.

Finance

Assess carefully the amount of finance needed:

> to buy fixed assets;
> to pay start-up costs;
> to fund working capital.

The most reliable way of making this assessment is to prepare a Cash Flow Forecast. However, this is not a 'crystal ball' to forecast the future. It is:

1. *Standing costs* A detailed statement of standing costs showing what cash will have to be spent in each of the first 12 months of trading. This defines the gross profit to be earned.
2. *Net sales* A projection of possible sales and income therefrom and the direct costs to be met in securing them, also in each of the first 12 months. This assesses the capability of earning gross profit.
3. *Trading surplus deficit* The difference between standing costs and net sales identifies the cash surplus or deficit on trading in each month and progressively through the year. This is the working capital requirement.
4. *Capital expenditure* A detailed statement of the cost of purchasing and installing fixed assets and the legal or other costs of incorporating the business, phased according to expected time for purchase and payment.
5. *Cash flow* The combination of trading surplus or deficit and capital expenditure shows the projected cash balance or overdraft for each month and progressively through the year.
6. *Funding need* The maximum overdraft or deficit shown in the progressive cash flow represents the amount of funds needed to support the enterprise.

Standing costs

This forecast can be remarkably close to reality because these are under the control of the business. Having assessed them carefully and in some detail, a *target* will have been set – a target for gross profit.

Be completely satisfied that standing costs have not been underestimated. Sales can be achieved to yield a gross profit which will be in excess of the standing costs.

If not so satisfied, revert to the business plan to see if there are any options which might prove more satisfactory.

If still not certain give up the idea altogether and look for another project.

Cash flow forecast

Page 1

Sole trader working from home

MONTH	1	2	3	4	5	6	7	Year
Standing costs								
Wages	160	160	200	160	160	200	160	2,080
Rent								—
Rates								—
Insurances	200							200
Telephone			55			55		220
Stationery	100							100
Power								52
Accountant	100							100
Vehicle – tax	150							150
insurance	55	55	55	55	55	55	55	658
fuel	10	10	10	10	10	10	10	120
Sundry								
Own drawings	500	500	500	500	500	500	500	6,000
£	1,275	725	820	725	725	820	725	9,680

Note

Costs	£9,680
Add:	
Depreciation	
on plant 10%	80
on vehicles 20%	240
Total	£10,000

To preserve own drawings at £6,000
Gross profit must be £10,000
To make a profit it must exceed £10,000
Are you sure you can make enough sales to achieve such a gross profit?

Cash flow forecast

Page 2

MONTH	1	2	3	4	5	6	7	Year 1	Year 2	Year 3
Standing costs (brought forward)	1,275	725	820	725	725	820	725	9,680	9,680	9,680
Sales invoiced	600	700	900	700	800	1,160	940	11,000	13,000	15,000
Income – cash	410	415	475	250	360	688	461	5,000	4,500	4,000
debtors		95	235	355	440	445	456	4,140	6,525	7,580
Direct cost	410	510	710	605	800	1,133	917	9,140	11,025	11,580
	30	35	45	35	40	58	47	550	650	750
Net Income	380	475	665	570	760	1,075	870	8,590	10,375	10,830
Cash flow from trading	(895)	(250)	(155)	(255)	35	255	145	(1,090)	695	1,150
Add: Govt Enterprise Allowance	160	160	200	160	160	200	160	2,080	—	—
Net Surplus (Deficit)	(735)	(90)	45	(95)	195	455	305	990	695	1,150
Capital purchases Vehicle	1,200							1,200		
Equipment	800							800		
Funds needed	2,735	2,825	2,780	2,875	2,680	2,225	1,920	1,010	315	(835)
Funds provided from: Own resources	1,000									
Grant/Loan	1,000									
Cash at bank Bank overdraft (before loan interest)	735	825	780	875	680	225	80	990	1,685	2,835

Net sales

Try to estimate how quickly sales could develop. Perhaps one should estimate on the most optimistic basis and the most pessimistic and test the implications of both on the trading surplus or deficit.

Make due allowance for late payment by customers but do not presume too much credit from suppliers unless there is already a good credit understanding.

Most new ventures take longer to establish than one supposes. Except in some unusual circumstances the outside world does not share your enthusiasm and does not beat a path to your door.

In plotting direct costs do not overlook or underestimate the need for *stocks* whenever they are necessary to provide quick deliveries. Stock holdings are a question of a fine balance – an over-estimate of demand can bring financial disaster and yet an inability to supply can lose a market.

Capital expenditure

Consider whether new or used plant is most appropriate having regard to the short term running costs of each and the productivity capabilities.

Present the establishment to the market in the most impressive way that can be afforded. Consider the initial requirements for plant and equipment and whether some items can be left until subsequent phases of development. Do not over-elaborate at the outset but do not kill the project with caution.

Having completed one year's cash flow project the Profit and Loss Account and Balance Sheet as at the end of year 1 and repeat the whole exercise for year 2 and year 3 to test its longer term viability.

For year 2 and 3 it is sufficient to work on annual rather than monthly figures.

A useful test for an expansion programme is to discover how long it will take to accumulate enough profit to pay off the investment – the pay-back period – three years is satisfactory in most circumstances – more than three years becomes suspect.

Remember that expenses and income must be recorded in the month when it will arise – taking account of credit allowed or received and whether expenses will be incurred monthly, quarterly or periodically.

A cash flow forecast is exactly that – cash flow – when money is expected to come into and go out of the business.

Sources of funding

1. Government and local authorities
May offer grants, loans or subsidies frequently related to job creation.
Enquire at:
Department of Trade & Industry
Economic Development Department or the local authority
any development agency

2. Clearing banks

May offer loans or overdraft facilities	Frequently need security

3. Other institutions

Merchant banks	Usually need security
Pension Funds	
Venture Capital Trusts	May want a shareholding
Insurance Companies	

4. Hire purchasing and leasing

To finance capital expenditure	May need additional security in the form of a personal guarantee

5. Factoring or invoice discounting

For fee, a factor will advance money against book debts	Factor takes over the sales ledger, credit control and debt collection
	Invoice discounting leaves these functions with the business and the bad debt risk

People and institutions lend in the hope of getting a reward. The business or expansion plan must excite them. They will look to the business to provide some funds and share the risks.

Fund raising may influence, or be influenced by, the structure of the business. Limited companies and partnerships can sometimes offer more tangible security than private individuals or sole traders. Get advice from a solicitor or an accountant.

Business structures

A sole trader
  is in complete control to do as he pleases;
  he owns the whole business;
  the profit is his –
  but so are the liabilities and the risk.

A partnership
  partners own and control the business jointly;
  the profit is shared;
  and so are the liabilities and the risks – but if one partner defaults those remaining are responsible for his share of liabilities.
  The business may benefit from the pooling of knowledge and experience.
  A *partnership agreement* should be drawn up by a solicitor to define partners' rights, duties and the basis of sharing the profits.

A limited company
  is a body created by a group of people (could be husband and wife) each of whom has a share in it – shareholders.
  The company is controlled by directors appointed by the shareholders and can do only as authorised by its Memorandum and Articles of Association.
  All assets belong to the company.
  The risk ultimately rests with the shareholders but their liability is limited – once they have subscribed the price of their shares they have no further liability.
  All profit belongs to the company but it may be distributed to the shareholders as dividend.
  The conduct of the company is governed by legislation.

Formalities

Sole trader
  none, other than notifying Inland Revenue, Department of Social Services and registering for VAT if applicable.

Partnership
  as with a sole trader but, to protect all concerned, a partnership agreement should be drawn up in writing.

Limited company

has to be registered with the Registrar of Companies. Its Memorandum and Articles of Association, defining its objects and specifying the rights and conduct of shareholders and directors, must be in accordance with company legislation which also lays down the way in which financial accounts are presented and audited by an accountant.

Can be created quite inexpensively, but a solicitor must be involved.

Taxation

Sole trader

pays tax on the profit of the business; is not paid a salary by the business but may take drawings which are regarded as advances of profit.

Partners

are taxable on their share of the profits in the same way as sole traders;

may be paid salaries, which are deducted from the partnership profits, but are taxable on the partners.

Limited company

pays corporation tax on its profit (before distribution of dividend); directors may receive salaries and, like other employees, are subject to PAYE;

shareholders suffer income tax on dividends.

Security

Compared with a sole trader:

The broader base of knowledge and experience of the partners may appear a more safe investment to a potential lender.

A limited company can offer shares in the business as security, or charge its fixed and floating assets (stock, debtors and cash) under a debenture which gives the lender first call on them in the event of liquidation or winding up.

Chapter 6

Financial Control

Financing investment

Financial control is all about control of cash-flow.

Make sure money goes out of the business and comes in as and when it should and in a way which maximises cash-in-hand or at the bank. The conduct of a business is a series of investment decisions. Investment in:

buildings, plant and equipment;
people;
ideas and projects.

Building, plant and equipment
Weigh up the pros and cons of purchasing as against renting, leasing, lease purchase or hire-purchase.

If some capital is available it may be preferable to purchase against a partial mortgage because even part ownership can be useful security for a short-time borrowing to meet needs as they arise.

Leasing, lease or hire-purchase can be expensive but may be tax effective and avoids capital outlay.

Fixed assets work for the business – make sure that you are not over-equipped, but that all your assets are as fully used as possible and are maintained so as to operate at their designed efficiency and output rate. Note that operating plant on shift working may avoid outlay on plant and buildings, but unless the plant is very expansive the operating costs per unit of output may well rise and the profit per unit may fall.

People
Employ the most competent staff you can afford, spend time and money training them well and be sure that they work efficiently.

Ideas and projects

Evaluate by detailed plans and cash flow projections, test thoroughly the commercial viability and the return on the investment as opposed to other possible alternatives before proceeding.

Working capital

Is stock moving or turning over quickly enough and are debtors paying on time so that money is not being locked up needlessly when it could be earning a return in some alternative investment? Is cash surplus to immediate requirements being invested?

1. Amounts of £5,000/£10,000 can usually be invested overnight to return next morning.
2. Cash received from customers early in the month may not be needed until it is time to pay suppliers. It can be invested 'on call' and called in when such cheques are written.
3. Cash required to pay inevitable VAT or tax can be set aside monthly to earn interest until payments are due.

Exercising control

Control should be exercised over the following:
    the budget;
    short term cash flow;
    monthly management accounts;
    credit control;
    economic indicators.

The budget

This should be prepared each year and take the form of a monthly or quarterly forecast of cash flow, Profit and Loss Account and Balance Sheet. It could be not so much a forecast as a target.

In bigger companies separate budgets or targets should be prepared by the various departments covering their own areas of responsibility, ie Sales, Marketing, Research and Development, Production Departments and Administration. These separate budgets will then be consolidated to form a company budget or target.

The budget should not confine itself to wholly financial objectives. Sales budgets may include a target to open so many new accounts.

Production budgets may include a target to increase saleable output per man-hour. Administration budget may include a target to reduce the average debtors' period to 45 days.

The budget should answer the questions:

What do we want to achieve this year?
What achievements will persuade us to say 'that was a good year'?

It should not be put away in a drawer but used as a navigation chart.

As each month goes by, compare actual achievements with budget and ask:

If we are not where we meant to be – why not?
Are we better off or worse off?
Should we alter course?

If a change of course is needed – perhaps because of unforeseeable circumstances, prepare a revised budget.

Short-term cash flow

At the beginning of each month one knows what debtors are outstanding and, based on the track record of customers, can take a view of the money receivable in each of the next eight weeks. Similarly one knows what wages and creditors have to be paid. Cash flow for eight weeks can thus be anticipated with some accuracy. This knowledge will be vital in deciding what short term commitments may be undertaken and the best use to which available cash can be put.

The order book and general state of trading may permit a calculated estimation of the likely cash flow for a further period ahead – if sales and purchasing requirements are clearly defined – a 12- or even 16-week forecast of cash flow is even more helpful than one for eight weeks.

Short term cash forecasting should be a regular habit and if income is not arriving as anticipated questions must be answered.

Management accounts

Each month, or at least every three months, prepare a Trial Balance to show the trading result of the month, the financial year to date and the Balance Sheet as at the end of the month. Compare the results with the budget and investigate the deviations in income and expenditure on each account. Focus attention on the three fundamentals of the Profit and Loss Account: direct cost; gross profit; and standing cost.

The essentials of the Balance Sheet are:

current assets/liabilities – the liquidity ratio;
capital employed and return on capital.

Due perhaps to seasonal influences, a budget is sometimes better prepared on a quarterly rather than a monthly basis. But management should still be prepared monthly to monitor progress towards the quarterly total – or identify what remains to be done.

Credit control and debt collection

Investigate and confirm credit rating of customer before extending credit. Enquire of credit agencies, ask to see recent accounts, take up trade and bank references. Allowing credit is an investment in your customer – make sure it will be repaid.

Assess how much credit the business is prepared to risk – the credit limit – on each customer.

Before undertaking any order, check that its value, plus the value of any outstanding invoices, is within the customer's credit limit. If not – ask for some payment before accepting the order.

Send out invoices on the day of despatch or at least the next day.

Collect debts promptly.

If invoices not paid, when:

1 week overdue	send reminder letter.
2 weeks overdue	send stronger reminder and telephone customer.
4 weeks overdue	stop supplies and threaten legal action may have to be taken.
5 weeks overdue	give 7 days' notice of legal action.
6 weeks overdue	call in solicitor or debt-collection agency or for smaller claims, issue a County Court writ.

This programme may sound tough, but you have earned the money and need it to finance your business – you cannot afford to finance your customers beyond the amount of credit you have agreed.

Always consider your customer's problems, if he explains them to you, and negotiate agreeable terms for settlement. Settlement or cash discounts are an expensive way of debt collecting. Remember that giving 2½ per cent discount for payment in seven days to a customer who usually takes 45 days, means that to receive your money 38 days sooner you are paying the equivalent of 24 per cent per annum interest. It may only be worth while in most exceptional circumstances.

Conditions of sale

Consider carefully the terms upon which you wish to trade. The main points to be covered are:

on what conditions can you be held to your price quotations or price lists;
when does ownership of the goods you sell pass to the customer?
what is your liability for damages to or caused by the goods you sell?
and there will be several other matters relating to your particular trade or profession which need to be clarified before you do business.

Seek advice from a solicitor or trade association
Make your conditions clear to your customer before you accept an order to avoid doubt and misunderstanding in the event of trouble, for your defence should legal action be taken against you and to safeguard your rights should your customer go into bankruptcy or liquidation whilst still owing you money.

Economic indicators

Apart from those already mentioned, arising out of the Profit and Loss Account and the Balance Sheet there are a number of other economic indicators. These are outlined below.

Aged debtors analysis
Each month, prepare a list of debtors and identify the age of each debtor's balance (the months in which the constituent invoices were sent). Examine closely those debts which are overdue and review debt collecting.

A useful control is to assess debtors in terms of the average number of days of credit being taken by customers.

Example
Suppose a business allows customers 30 days' credit. It will expect payment, on average, in 45 days.

Assume the following is extracted from the books as at 31 October.

Month	Sales £	Debtors at 31 Oct £	Days in month	Days of sales in debtors
October	5,000	4,500	31	27.9
September	4,000	2,000	30	15.0
August	6,000	1,000	31	5.2
Actual days of sales in debtors				48.1

Something should be done to speed up payments by some debtors.

Aged creditors analysis

Each month, prepare a list of all creditors and identify the age of each balance (the months in which the constituent invoices were received). Examine particularly the creditors to whom your payments are overdue and do something about them. If you cannot pay, explain your position to them and try to negotiate settlement terms before they lose patience and send you a writ.

Operating efficiency report

Keep records which will enable you to compare actual time taken on jobs (including stoppages and lost time) with your estimate of the times which should have been taken. This will help in making future estimates and quotations more realistic.

Examine the causes of stoppages and other lost time and try to take action to avoid re-occurrencies:

$$\frac{\text{Estimate time}}{\text{Actual time}} \times 100 = \text{Efficiency \% (it should be over 80 at least)}$$

If possible, review efficiency of individual people and individual machines, or of each department, but, if nothing else, for the business as a whole.

Another useful guide is to calculate and review production or sales per person or per man-hour employed.

Statistics on stoppages of machines or of break-down time lost can focus on the need for better maintenance programmes or for replacements.

Records of absence, time-keeping and efficiency of people can help identify a need for training, job changes or staff changes.

Chapter 7
Worked Examples

Cash Book

	RECEIPTS							PAYMENTS					
Date		Received from	Total Rec'd	VAT %	VAT	Net	Date		Paid to	Total paid	VAT %	VAT	Net
Oct	19	B. Smith	21.15	17.5	3.15	18.00	Oct	19	Lunch	4.30			4.30
									Petrol	9.20	17.5	1.37	7.83
	20	Mrs Black	65.80	17.5	9.80	56.00		20	Coffee	1.94			1.94
	22	Johnson	28.20	17.5	4.20	24.00		23	Lunch	4.75			4.75
	23	Jones	15.27	17.5	2.27	13.00							
										20.19		1.37	18.82
									Net takings Banked 23.10.87	110.23		18.05	92.18
			130.42		19.42	111.00				130.42		19.42	111.00
A/c							A/c						
100		Cash Sales	111.00				412		Vehicle expenses	7.83			
732		VAT Output	19.42				409		Office expenses	10.99			
							732		VAT Input	1.37			
			130.42							20.19			

If the amount of VAT is not shown separately on your bills for purchases or sales it must be calculated.

Example:

If VAT rate is 17.5 per cent your payment or receipt equals 117.5 per cent of the price excluding VAT

Thus VAT = 17.5/117.5ths of the amount paid or received.

Bank Book

Left-hand side

RECEIPTS

Date		Received from	Total Rec'd	Disc Allowed	Total	CR sales 620	Cash Sales 101									VAT %	VAT 732
Oct	1	Brought fwd			124.40												
	9	Cash	206.60				206.60										
	14	Watson Smith	2385.45														
		Jones	1710.80														
		Pike	969.37			5065.42											
			(5065.42)														
	16	Cash	125.45				125.45										
	20	Wardridge	58.75			58.75											
	23	Cash	110.23				110.23										
	28	Coombe	145.70														
		Cameron	896.52			1042.42											
			(1042.42)														
	30	Cash	87.00				87.00										
		Total Rec'd	6695.87														
					6820.27	6166.59	529.28										

Right-hand side

PAYMENTS

Date	Chq No	Paid to	Total Paid	Disc Rec'd	Total	CR Purch	Net pay 720	Ded'ns 722	PAYE 721	HM Customs 732	Fixed Assets 301/5	Draw'gs 420	Sundry	VAT %	VAT 732
Oct															
2	436	Box – landlord	100.00			100.00									
14	437	Revenue	358.33						358.33						
28	438	Brown	142.00				142.00								
	439	Hood	178.00				178.00								
	440	Robinson	200.00				200.00								
	441	T.S.B.	30.00					30.00							
29	442	Daleside	1786.00			1786.00									
	443	BNK Eng.	883.60			883.60									
	444	Atkinson	1703.75			1703.75									
	445	Waldorf	387.75			387.75									
30	446	Self	500.00									500.00			
	447	Elec. Board	109.43			109.43									
	448	G.P.O.	72.85			72.85									
	449	S.M.T. Garage	64.63			64.63									
	450	Kidd	68.38			68.38									
	D.D.	Bank charges	12.00										12.00		
	S.O.	Rates	100.00			100.00									
		Balance c/fwd			123.55										
			6696.72		6820.27	5276.39	520.00	30.00	358.33			500.00	12.00		

109

Bank reconciliation
as at 31 October

	£
Balance per bank statement	851.84
Add: deposits in Bank Book but not on Statement	
30 October Cash	87.00
	938.84
Deduct: Cheques in Bank Book but not on Statement	
Cheques 446–450	815.29
Balance per Bank Book	123.55

Invoice

INVOICE   No. 678

A & B TRADERS
14 South Street, Newcastle Upon Tyne NE3 1BT

VAT Reg. No. 403 3580 86   Date: 17 August 1994

Customer:

Watson Smith & Sons
82 Field Street
Warchester

Description	Quantity	Price			£	
Mild steel gadgets	150	4.20	630	00		
Stainless steel widgets	150	4.50	675	00		
Bright steel closure rings	100	7.25	725	00		
					2,030	00
					2,030	00
VAT at 17.5%					355	25
Total £					2,385	25

Terms of payment: Net 30 days from date of Invoice.
Interest at 2% per month will be charged
on overdue accounts.

Sales book

	SALES								
Date	Inv No	Customer	Inv Total	VAT	NET	Am't paid	Date	Method	
Aug									
17	678	W. Smith	2385.25	355.25	2030.00	2385.25	14/10	Cheque	
18	679	Jones	1710.80	254.80	1456.00	1710.80	14/10	,,	
19	680	Archibald	299.62	44.62	255.00				
24	681	Pike	969.37	144.37	825.00	969.37	14/10	Cheque	
26	682	Ward	58.75	8.75	50.00	58.75	20/10	,,	
27	683	Coombe	145.70	21.70	124.00	145.70	28/10	,,	
27	684	Cameron	896.53	133.53	763.00	896.53	28/10	,,	
27	685	Rogers	405.38	60.38	345.00				
28	686	Black	881.25	131.25	750.00				
			7752.65	1154.65	6598.00				
Sep									
20	687	Smith	1762.50	262.50	1500.00				
20	688	Ward	734.38	109.38	625.00				
22	689	Cameron	940.00	140.00	800.00				
23	690	Coombe	293.75	43.75	250.00	287.50	30/9	Cheque	
23	691	Pike	2643.75	393.75	2250.00	2587.50	30/9	,,	
			6374.38	949.38	5425.00				
Oct									
22	692	Smith	2996.25	446.25	2550.00				
22	693	Ward	763.75	113.75	650.00				
	694	Coombe	1233.75	183.75	1050.00				
	695	Jones	1468.75	218.75	1250.00				
			6462.50	962.50	5500.00				
		TOTALS							

Ledger account

Name	Watson Smith & Sons	Contact: Oscar Smith
Address	82 Field Street	
	Warchester	Phone: 043 46247

Account No. 1

Credit Limit £10,000

Date	Invoice or Cheque No	Brief Details	Dr		Cr		Balance	
Aug 17	678	Spares	2385	.25			2385	.25
Sep 20	687	Spares	1762	.50			4147	.75
Oct 14	084	Cheque			2385	.25	1762	.50
Oct 22	692	Type D containers	2996	.25			4758	.75

Overdue list

No.	ACCOUNT Name	TOTAL BALANCE	Analysis of balance Current	1 month Overdue	2 months Overdue	3 months Overdue	4 months Overdue	5 months Overdue
1	Watson Smith	4758.75	2996.25	1762.50				
2	Crawford Jones	1468.75	1468.75					
3	James Pike							
4	Jonathon Ward	1498.12	763.75	734.37				
5	A. J. Coombe	1233.75	1233.75					
6	Marshall Cameron	940.00		940.00				
7	Arnold Rogers	405.38			405.38			
8	Joseph Black	881.25			881.25			
9	R. Archibald	299.62			299.62			
		11,485.62	6462.50	3436.87	1586.87			

Purchases book

PURCHASES

Date	Supplier	Inv Total	VAT	NET	Am't paid	Date	Method	Raw mat'ls 201	Rent 417	Rates 417	Tel 408	Power 403	Vehicle 412	Ptg 407
Sep	Daleside	1786.00	266.00	1520.00		29/10	Cheque	1520.00						
	BNK	883.60	131.60	752.00		,,	,,	752.00						
	Atkinson	1703.75	253.75	1450.00		,,	,,	1450.00						
	Waldorf	387.75	57.75	330.00		,,	,,	330.00						
	Elec Bd	109.43	16.30	93.13		30/10	Cheque					93.13		
	PO	72.85	10.85	62.00		,,	,,				62.00			
	SMT	64.63	9.63	55.00		,,	,,						55.00	
	Kidd	68.38	10.18	58.20		2/10	Cheque							58.20
	Box	100.00		100.00		30/10	S.O.		100.00					
	UDC	100.00		100.00						100.00				
		5276.39	756.06	4520.33				4052.00	100.00	100.00	62.00	93.13	55.00	58.20
Oct	Daleside	1175.00	175.00	1000.00				1000.00						
	Atkinson	705.00	105.00	600.00				600.00						
	Waldorf	70.50	10.50	60.00				60.00						
	Schapp	311.38	46.38	265.00				265.00						
	Box	100.00		100.00					100.00					
	UDC	100.00		100.00						100.00				
	TOTALS	2461.88	336.88	2125.00				1925.00	100.00	100.00				

115

Reconciliation of creditors

OCTOBER

	£
Creditors at 30 Sept	8,264.88
+ Purchases ex-Purchases Book	2,461.88
	762.76
− Payments ex-Bank Book	276.39
Creditors at 31 Oct	5,450.37

agrees with list of creditors balances in Creditors Ledger.

Reconciliation of debtors
OCTOBER

	£
Debtors at 30 Sept	11,190.71
+ Sales ex-Sales Book	6,462.50
	652.21
− Receipts ex-Bank Book	6,166.59
Debtors at 31 Oct	11,485.62

agrees with list of debtors per overdue list and Debtors' Ledger.

Wages payroll

WAGES

No	Name	Hours worked				Rate per hour	Gross pay	Adj	Taxable pay	Tax	NI	Other deductions		Total ded	Taxable pay less ded	Adj	Net pay	Er's NI
		Basic	O/T 1	O/T 2	Total							Save						
1	Brown B.H.	160			160	1.25	200.00		200.00	40.00	18.00			58.00	148.00		142.00	18.00
2	Hood J.	160			160	1.875	300.00		300.00	85.00	27.00	10.00		122.00	178.00		178.00	27.00
	Total wages	320			320		500.00		500.00	125.00	45.00	10.00		180.00	320.00		320.00	45.00
	Salaries: Robinson						333.33		333.33	83.33	30.00	20.00		133.33	200.00		200.00	30.00
	Total payroll						833.33			208.33	75.00	30.00		313.33			520.00	75.00

117

DO YOUR OWN BOOKKEEPING

Stock record

ITEM	Month September			Month October			Month		
	Qty	Price	Cost	Qty	Price	Cost	Qty	Price	Cost
Part No. 124	100	2.50	250.00	70	2.50	175.00			
No. 2 Widgets	248	3.20	793.60	180	3.20	576.00			
No. 3 Gadgets				83	3.00	249.00			
			1,043.60			1,000.00			
Work in progress									
Job No. 1235			450.00						
Job No. 1248						500.00			
Saleable stock									
Job No. 1226 Ward			650.00						
Job No. 1235 Pike						1,000.00			
TOTALS			2,143.60			2,500.00			

118

Register of fixed assets

Date of Purchase	Description of Asset	Exp-ected Life Years	Cost £	Year 1991		Year 1992		Year 1993		Year	
				Dep'n	Net Value	Dep'n	Net Value	Dep'n	Net Value	Dep'n	Net Value
1985	Ford car ABC 724V	4	1,500	375	1,125	375	750	375	375		
1986	Desk and chair	10	150			15	135	15	120		
1986	Filing cabinet	10	100			10	90	10	80		
1987	Typewriter	10	500					50	450		
	TOTALS			375	1,125	400	975	450	1,025		

Journal

JOURNAL							
Ref No	Account	Account No	Dr			Cr	
	Vehicle expenses	412	7	83			
	Office expenses	409	10	99			
	To: VAT	732	1	17		16	65
	Cash sales	100				3	34
			19	99		19	99
	Analysis of cash receipts and expenses for week ended 23.10.93						
	Direct wages (incl. employer's NI)	211	545	00			
	Salaries (incl. employer's NI)	302	363	33			
	To: PAYE/NI	721				358	33
	Other deductions	722				30	00
	Net pay	720				520	00
			908	33		908	33
	Payroll entries for the month of October						
	Stocks – materials	610	1,000	00			
	work in progress	611	500	00			
	saleable stock	612	1,000	00			
	To: Raw materials	201				2,500	00
			2,500	00		2,500	00
	Stocks entries at 31 October						
	Depreciation	499	37	50			
	To: Fixed assets	801				37	50
	Depreciation charge for the month of October						

Further Reading from Kogan Page

Budgeting: A Practical Guide for Better Business Planning, Terry Dickey, 1992

The Business Plan Workbook, Colin Barrow, Paul Barrow and Robert Brown, 2nd edition, 1992

Customer Service, Malcolm Peel, 1987

Financial Management for the Small Business, Colin Barrow, 3rd edition, 1995

How to Sell More! Neil Johnson, 1994

The Small Business Action Kit, 4th edition, J Rosthorn and others, 1994

Business Basics series

Be Your Own Accountant, Philip McNeill and Sarah JP Howarth

Budgeting for Business, Leon Hopkins

Business Cash Books Made Easy, Max Pullen

Business Plans, Brian Finch

Cash Flow and How to Improve It, Leon Hopkins

Controlling Costs, John F Gittus

Costing Made Easy, Graham Mott

Pricing for Profit, Gregory Lewis

Taxes on Business, Kevin Armstrong